D0791198

SPORT PSYCHOLOGY LIBRARY:

BASKETBALL

Praise for Sport Psychology Library:
BASKETBALL

John Wooden, Basketball Hall of Fame Player and Coach

"Having known Dale Brown for many years, I'm quite sure that those interested in improving their knowledge and enjoyment of the sport of basketball will acquire immeasurable insights on a much-overlooked part of the game. Coach Brown is a real student of the game and he has excellent ability to convey his thoughts to others. Too often we think of just the physical skills of basketball, but the physical skills are dependent on the mental side. Coach Brown gets this idea across very clearly in Sport Psychology Library: Basketball."

Bill Walton, Basketball Hall of Fame Player

"Coach Dale Brown is a visionary leader and teacher who has captured the spirit of the world's highest level of competition: basketball and its relationship to your personal life. Thank you, Dale, for making it all real and so crystal clear."

Rick Barry, Basketball Hall of Fame Player

"I thoroughly enjoyed reading this book and discovered many valuable techniques, which are definitely worth utilizing by players, coaches and parents. Many of the techniques I had learned on my own after many years of playing and coaching. I especially enjoyed the FUNdamental Points to Remember section of the book. After all, sports is supposed to be fun and this book will help make that a reality."

Shaquille O'Neal, 2-time LSU All-American, named one of NBA's 50 Greatest Players

"Dale Brown's knowledge of the game is legendary. He gave me knowledge I still use today."

Dr. Robert Weinberg, Miami University, Editor-in-Chief, Journal of Applied Sport Psychology, voted one of the top ten sport psychology specialists in North America by his peers.

"The authors have combined research and practical experience in this easy to read and informative book on sport psychology and basketball. It's a must read for players, coaches, and parents alike who are interested in the mental side of basketball."

SPORT PSYCHOLOGY LIBRARY:

BASKETBALL

Kevin L. Burke
Dale Brown

Fitness Information Technology, Inc.
P.O. Box 4425, University Avenue
Morgantown, WV 26504-4425 USA

The sport psychological techniques or physical activities discussed in this book are not intended as a substitute for consultation with a sport psychologist or physician. Further, because people respond differently, it cannot be guaranteed that these psychological techniques will result in an improvement in sport performance. Readers are encouraged to contact the Association for the Advancement of Applied Sport Psychology, the American Psychological Association, or the United States Olympic Committee for further information about the delivery of sport psychology services.

Copyright © 2003, by Kevin L. Burke and Dale Brown

ALL RIGHTS RESERVED

Reproduction or use of any portion of this publication by any mechanical, electronic, or other means is prohibited without the written permission of the publisher.

Library of Congress Card Catalog Number: 2002102134

ISBN: 1-885693-37-0

Copyeditor: Sandra Woods
Cover Design: James R. Bucheimer
Developmental Editor: Geoffrey C. Fuller
Production Editor: Craig R. Hines
Assistant Editor: Jessica McDonald
Proofreader: Candace Jordan
Indexer: Maria denBoer
Printed by: Data Reproductions Corporation

Printed in the United States of America
10   9   8   7   6   5   4   3   2   1

Fitness Information Technology, Inc.
P.O. Box 4425, University Avenue
Morgantown, WV 26504 USA
800.477.4348
304.599.3483
Email: fit@fitinfotech.com
Web Site: www.fitinfotech.com

About the Sport Psychology Library

Basketball is another outstanding addition to the Sport Psychology Library series. This is the first series that combines the skills and experiences of athletes and sport psychologists to show athletes, coaches, and parents how to get the most from their sports involvement. Each book in the series focuses on a specific sport so your special questions and needs can be directly addressed. Renowned coach Dale Brown and esteemed sport psychologist Kevin Burke bring you the third book in the series, *Basketball*. Their combined expertise offers you everything you need to become an outstanding and consistently successful basketball player. Not only is this book filled with useful tips and strategies for mastering the mental game of basketball, but it's fun to read!

Now, it's time for me to get out of the way so you can enjoy this wonderful book!

Shane Murphy, Ph.D.
Editor-in-Chief
Sport Psychology Library

Dr. Shane Murphy is the former head of the Sport Psychology Department of the United States Olympic Committee and is currently President of Gold Medal Psychological Consultants.

Photo Credits

Page 7: Photo copyright of Georgia Southern University. Reprinted with permission.

Page 11: Photo copyright of Georgia Southern University. Reprinted with permission.

Page 17: Photo copyright of Georgia Southern University. Reprinted with permission.

Page 41: Photo copyright of Georgia Southern University. Reprinted with permission.

Page 43: Photo copyright of John Bright and Bright Images Photography. Reprinted with permission.

Page 49: Photo copyright of Georgia Southern University. Reprinted with permission.

Page 57: Photo copyright of Georgia Southern University. Reprinted with permission.

Page 61: Photo copyright of John Bright and Bright Images Photography. Reprinted with permission.

Page 67: Photo copyright of Georgia Southern University. Reprinted with permission.

Page 74: Photo copyright of Barry A. Munkasy. Reprinted with permission.

Page 76: Photo copyright of WVU Photography. Reprinted with permission.

Page 91: Photo copyright of Georgia Southern University. Reprinted with permission.

Page 97: Photo copyright of Georgia Southern University. Reprinted with permission.

Page 105: Photo copyright of Georgia Southern University. Reprinted with permission.

About the Authors

Coach Dale Brown

Dale Brown, one of the outstanding personalities in college athletics, began his 44-year coaching career as a high school wrestling, football, and track coach. He served as an assistant coach for 5 years at Utah State and 1 year at Washington State before becoming head coach at Louisiana State University. In the 25 years before Brown's arrival, LSU won 288 games and went to 2 NCAA tournaments. Under Brown's coaching, game attendance soared and the Tigers won 448 games and appeared in 13 NCAA tournaments. His 1986 team was the lowest seed (11th) to ever advance to the Final Four. Only one other coach in the Southeastern Conference won more games than Brown, whose team won or were the runners-up at the SEC conference 8 times during a 14-year span. Coach Brown is the only SEC coach to appear in 15 straight national tournaments, and he was voted SEC Coach of the year multiple times. He was also selected as the Louisiana College Basketball Coach of the year 7 times. In 1981, *Sporting News* and the NBC sports staff named Brown the National Basketball Coach of the year, and *Playboy* magazine selected Coach Brown as their 1988 College Coach of the year. In recent years, Coach Brown has become an author and motivational speaker.

Kevin L. Burke

Kevin L. Burke is an associate professor and the graduate program director of the Department of Health & Kinesiology at Georgia Southern University. He is also the program coordinator for the graduate program in sport psychology and director of the Sport Psychology Laboratory at GSU. He received a BA in psychology and recreational studies (double major) with a minor in sociology from Belmont

Abbey College in 1982. Dr. Burke was a member of the Pi Gamma Mu National Social Science Honor Society. He also played on the men's tennis team and was a National Association of Intercollegiate Athletics Academic All-American Tennis Team nominee, making the NAIA All-District 26 Tennis Team in both singles and doubles play. Dr. Burke received his MA in social/organizational psychology from East Carolina University in 1984, where he was a member of Psi Chi, the National Honor Society in psychology. He earned his PhD in sport psychology from Florida State University in 1988. Dr. Burke is currently on the editorial board of the Journal of Applied Sport Psychology and has edited and reviewed for several other journals.

Contents

Pre-Game: How Players, Coaches, and Parents
Can Use This Book xv

Section I: ***FUN*damental Basketball**

Chapter 1:   Basketball—Much More Than Physical Skills 3

Chapter 2:   *FUN*damental Skills of the Complete
Basketball Player 9

Section II: **Assisting Yourself With Mental Skills**

Chapter 3:   Shooting. 37

Chapter 4:   Playing Defense 47

Chapter 5:   Becoming a Better All-Around Player 55

Chapter 6:   Sporting Behavior: Being a Good "Sport" 65

Chapter 7:   Dealing With Referees, Fans, Opponents,
Injuries, and Other Situations. 73

Chapter 8:   Staying Motivated. 85

Chapter 9:   Gaining and Maintaining Confidence. 95

Chapter 10:   Playing in the Fun Zone 103

Appendix: Basketball-Related Web Sites 109

Index: 111

Acknowledgments

Thanks to all my players, players' parents, assistant coaches, associates, friends, and family for your trust.

—D.B.

I would like to acknowledge the staff at Fitness Information Technology, Inc., for helping to make this book a reality. I appreciate their feedback and positive attitudes toward completing this "labor of love."

I especially want to thank the editor, Shane Murphy, for his keen insights and suggestions during the writing process. His sound, concise comments definitely improved this book.

I am indebted to all of the past teachers, coaches, teammates, friends, students, and basketball officials I have had the opportunity to work with for sharing their knowledge of psychology and/or basketball with me. In particular, I considered it an honor getting to know and work with Coach Dale Brown on this project. Coach Brown is one of the most optimistic persons I have ever met.

I send thanks to my family for continuing to be important to my development as a person. I will always be grateful to my late father, Norman, for introducing me to basketball and sharing his love for this great sport with me. Dad, I miss our one-on-one games in the driveway.

Finally, I want to thank my lifetime "teammate" and favorite basketball player—my wife, Shelly. Your encouragement, support, and love are more than I could have ever wished for.

—K.L.B.

Detailed Contents

Pre-Game: How Players, Coaches, and Parents
Can Use This Book xv

The Book's Relevance for Players xvi

The Book's Relevance for Coaches xvi

The Book's Relevance for Parents xvii

Section I: *FUN*damental Basketball 1

Chapter 1:   Basketball—Much More Than Physical Skills 3

Scouting Report 3

Playing Percentages 3

*FUN*damental Skills 4

The Mental Side of Basketball 5

*FUN*damental Points to Remember 8

Chapter 2:   *FUN*damental Skills of the
Complete Basketball Player 9

Scouting Report 9

*FUN*damental Skill #1—Mental Practice 10

Understanding Mental Practice 12

Getting Started 13

When You Should Practice 14

Mental Practice Schedule 15

Mental Practice Notebook 15

Frequently Asked Questions About Imagery 17

Viewpoint 17

Control 18

Belief 18

Using Imagery During Games or Practice 18

*FUN*damental Skill #2—Concentration Awareness Training 19

Understanding Concentration. 20

The Specifics of Concentration. 20

Four Ways to Focus 21

Three Important Aspects of Concentration 22

Helpful Concentration Tips 24

Full-Court Concentration. 24

Concentration With Many Time-Outs (TOs). 24

Concentration With Few TOs 24

Concentration Practice 25

*FUN*damental Skill #3—Positive Self-Talk (Gem Talk) 28

Changing Thought Habits 29

Self-Talk Statements 31

Using a Sense of Humor 32

*FUN*damental Points to Remember 33

Section II: Assisting Yourself With Mental Skills 35

Chapter 3:   Shooting. 37

Scouting Report 37

How to Lessen "Basket Interference". 37

Imagery Practice for Shooting. 38

Concentration and Gem-Talk Keys for Shooting. 39

Mental Routine for Shooting Free Throws. 40

Mental and Physical Free Throw Shooting Routine 44

*FUN*damental Points to Remember 45

Chapter 4:   Playing Defense 47

Scouting Report 47

Using Mental Skills to Improve Defense. 47

Team Defense 48

1-On-1 Defense. 50

Using Self-Talk to Improve Defense 51

FUNdamental Points to Remember 53

Chapter 5: Becoming a Better All-Around Player 55

Scouting Report 55

Skill Improvement...................................... 55

Imagery 56

Concentration 58

Self-Talk 59

Skill Correction and Slumps 59

Using the "Off" Hand 60

*FUN*damental Points to Remember 63

Chapter 6: Sporting Behavior: Being a Good "Sport" 65

Scouting Report 65

Being a Good Sport...................................... 65

Trash Talking... 66

Special Trash-Talk Practice 69

Psych-Out Attempt 69

Emotional Control....................................... 70

The Three-Seconds Rule 71

*FUN*damental Points to Remember 72

Chapter 7: Dealing With Referees, Fans, Opponents,
Injuries, and Other Situations...................... 73

Scouting Report 73

Officials 74

Opposing Fans.. 76

Off-the-Court Situations 77

Teammates and Coaches................................. 78

Injury and Rehabilitation................................ 79

Mental Rehabilitation Imagery Scenario 80

How to Have Fun When You're Way Behind or Way Ahead....... 81

Sitting on the Bench 82

Changing Negative Statements to Positive Self-Talk 83

*FUN*damental Points to Remember 84

Chapter 8: Staying Motivated. 85

    Scouting Report 85

    Attitude Adjustment. 85

    Goal Setting 87

    Ultimate Imagery. 90

    Avoiding and Dealing With Burnout. 90

    *FUN*damental Points to Remember 94

Chapter 9: Gaining and Maintaining Confidence. 95

    Scouting Report 95

    Losing Confidence 96

    Gaining Confidence. 96

    Dealing With Pressure 99

    *FUN*damental Points to Remember 101

Chapter 10: Playing in the Fun Zone. 103

    Scouting Report 103

    Getting the Most From Playing Basketball 103

    Applying Your Basketball Skills to Life. 104

    *FUN*damental Points to Remember 107

Appendix: Basketball-Related Web Sites 109

Dr. Kevin L. Burke's Web Sites. 110

Index. 111

PRE-GAME:
How Players, Coaches, and Parents Can Use This Book

The purpose of this book is to help basketball players, coaches, and parents learn how to have fun practicing and improving psychological or mental skills in basketball. Rather than just hoping these skills will improve with experience, it is possible to learn how to better concentrate, control emotions, handle pressure, and improve other important psychological (and physical) basketball skills. We believe it is essential that players, coaches, and parents are aware of, and emphasize, the

Players Can Learn
- to improve physical skills
- to improve mental skills
- to use imagery during games and practice
- to use positive self-talk

Coaches Can Learn
- to help players improve physical skills
- to help players improve mental skills
- to integrate imagery-use into practices
- to use positive self-talk

Parents Can Learn
- to understand the physical and mental needs of players
- to help players practice imagery
- to support players' practice of psychological skills
- to be more effective role models by effectively managing their own emotions

techniques that are available to master the FUNdamental aspects of the challenging, yet exciting, sport of basketball. Before you begin reading chapter 1, be sure to read the roles players, parents, and coaches may play in psychological skill improvement for basketball.

Players

This basketball psychology book was written especially for you. The techniques described in the following chapters will show you ways you can improve your FUNdamental basketball skills *on your own*. After reading this book, you can use it as a manual for future reference. For example, let's say you play a game where you only make one of five free throws. You realize after the game that you couldn't seem to focus while on the line—seemingly thinking of everything except shooting the free throws. To help you get back on track, you can refer to or reread part or all of chapter 3 of this book. Using this book as a reference or "how-to" manual will help you to remember what you need to do in the future to continue to improve your mental basketball skills. Again, how much you improve your FUNdamental skills *depends upon you*. Coaches, teammates, and parents can assist you along the way, but it is really up to you to give a "full-court" effort. Remember, you have to take charge and go on the offensive to become a more complete basketball player—mentally and physically.

Coaches

This basketball book can help you help your players improve both the mental and physical skills of this great sport. While you can learn ways to make basketball more fun for you and your players, you can also learn to apply the FUNdamental skills to become a more complete coach. You will find that most of the examples given in this book are presented from the player's point of view. However, coaches can take these techniques and apply them to themselves (i.e., using self-talk to control your emotions) or to practice or game situations. For example, in chapter 2, the mental practice technique of imagery is presented. As a coach, you can design your practice sessions so players will have opportunities to attempt these imagery skills. By devoting practice time to the acquisition of a mental skill such as imagery, you will be showing them how important you believe it is to mentally practice. Also, your players will be more likely to practice imagery on their own if you show them it is an important and consistent part of basketball practice. As a coach, you can also use imagery to practice staying calm and focused when practices or games are not going as well as you expected.

You can also use the FUNdamental skills presented in this book as a reference guide to help you improve your coaching abilities. You may find it helpful to refer to a particular chapter or section as necessary. By knowing how to keep and regain your concentration, use imagery to practice coaching in various game situations, and use positive self-talk with yourself (and more encouraging talk with your players), you can make yourself a more effective influence on your team. If you employ positive self-talk, you can influence your players to use the same technique. The simple formula of "positive coaching" is this: "If coaches remain positive, then players will likely be positive." This will make the basketball experience more enjoyable for you and your players.

Parents

Parents will find this basketball book helpful for several reasons. First, in order to be supportive of your "favorite" basketball player, it is helpful to know the mental practice techniques available to players and coaches. If psychological basketball skills training is not a part of his/her current regimen, you could use this book to introduce these techniques. If your son or daughter already uses psychological basketball skills training, learning more about these techniques may enable you to help when s/he requests help (i.e., have an imagery session or create a list of rebound statements together). At the very least you can understand how s/he is trying to become a complete player. Through a parental understanding of the importance of the mental side of playing basketball, you can serve as a supportive influence, helping your son or daughter realize the potential impact of practicing these indispensable skills.

As parents you will also find that the FUNdamental skills presented in the upcoming chapters will have specific benefits for you. For example, chapter 2 discusses how self-talk influences players' and coaches' reactions and emotions. At times you may become very emotional while watching your daughter's or son's team during a game. Although showing support is important, it is imperative that you avoid going too far, doing or saying something you may regret. By using the suggestions in chapter 2, you can learn how to keep your emotions in check and use a sense of humor to keep a proper perspective. By practicing imagery and utilizing positive self-talk, you can be an influential role model for your "star" player.

*FUN*damental Basketball

SECTION I

Basketball, more than any other sport, is a team game ... about the thousands of small, unselfish acts, the sacrifices on the part of the players that result in team building.

—Dean Smith (Hall of Fame coach and head coach of the University of North Carolina men's basketball team, who led his teams to two NCAA championships and retired as the "winningest" coach in college basketball history)

1

BASKETBALL—MUCH MORE THAN PHYSICAL SKILLS

SCOUTING REPORT -CHAPTER ONE-

You will read how to

1. Incorporate mental skills into your game.

2. Practice and improve your mental skills.

3. Make practicing and improving mental skills fun.

Playing Percentages

Players and coaches agree that the mental side of basketball is extremely important. However, to be the best all-around player possible, you need to practice physical and mental skills. To truly succeed in basketball, you need 100% in physical skills and 100% effort in the mental skills. These go hand in hand. You need *both* to be the best player you can become. It is important to practice both mental and physical skills.

FUNDAMENTAL SKILLS

Physical	Psychological or Mental
■ dribbling and shooting with both hands	■ concentrating
■ passing	■ controlling anger
■ playing defense	■ retaining confidence
■ rebounding	■ dealing with pressure
	■ performing in the "clutch"

Practice habits were crucial to my development in basketball. I didn't play against the toughest competition in high school, but one reason I was able to do well in college was that I mastered the fundamentals. You've got to have them down before you can even think about playing.

—Larry Bird (Fifth all-time leading free-throw-shooting percentage {.886} in the NBA, former coach of the Indiana Pacers, 3-time NBA Most Valuable Player, 3-time NBA Champion, and Hall of Famer)

*FUN*damental Skills

The will to win is grossly overrated. The will to prepare is far more important.

—Bob Knight (Member of the Hall of Fame; coached the Indiana Hoosiers to three NCAA national championships, with an undefeated season in 1976 (32-0); and coached the 1984 U.S. Olympic team to the Gold Medal)

There are many fundamental physical basketball skills to be learned and mastered, such as dribbling and shooting with both hands, passing, playing defense, and rebounding. However, some of the most important fundamental skills of basketball that can be improved are often the ones most overlooked—psychological skills! Knowing how to concentrate, control your anger, regain or retain your confidence, deal with pressure, and perform in the "clutch" are all skills that must be learned in order for your physical skills to reach their potential. To improve your mental skills, you must first recognize

A common misconception is that psychological skills must occur naturally. In fact, these skills are under your control.

that they CAN be improved and practiced, learn HOW to practice them, and realize they can be practiced almost anytime and anywhere.

The first step necessary to start on the road to improvement is to realize that psychological skills CAN be improved. This is often a stumbling block to getting better at the mental side of basketball. Many players and coaches think that being able to concentrate or keep your confidence is a natural-born skill that cannot be changed. Others feel these skills may naturally develop over a period of time. However, a key point to remember is that *psychological skills are like physical skills—they must be practiced in order to be improved.* Consider this example. Your coach has told you that you need to improve your free throw shooting percentage. To get better from the "charity stripe," you probably spend extra time working on getting your rhythm from the line. This means shooting numerous extra free throws before, after, or outside of your regular team practice until you begin to see improvement. You recognize the need to improve, so you go out and devote some extra practice to becoming a more successful free throw shooter. Now consider that your coach tells you that you need to concentrate better while on the court. What would you do? Do you know of specific techniques that could help you improve your concentration? Or would you just try to concentrate better?

To improve your free throw shooting, you would do more than simply try to shoot free throws better. You would spend extra practice time in order to improve. If your concentration is lacking, then extra practice time should be devoted to improving your concentration skills, too.

The Mental Side of Basketball

Do you know any specific techniques or drills that can help you improve your concentration, build your confidence, or handle pressure? If you answered "No" to this question, this book is perfect for you. Many coaches and athletes don't know how to work on their mental approach to basketball. That's why we wrote this book for you. The purpose of this book is to help you learn some mental exercises that will help you become stronger at the mental side of your game and become a complete basketball player. Becoming a psychologically sound basketball player is "FUN-to-mental." In other words, psychological skills are "fundamental" to the sport. It also can be fun to practice and improve your mental game. Advancing in the development of your physical skills without improving your

> Mastering your mental skills allows you to enjoy playing—whether you win or lose.

mental skills is like going through the aggravation of dribbling the length of the court to attempt a layup, then missing the uncontested shot. Mental skills can make the difference between success and failure and, just as important, can affect the amount of enjoyment you get from playing this great sport.

By mastering the mental side of basketball, you can insure your enjoyment of playing the game no matter what the game outcome may be. Even when your team doesn't score the most points, the mental game presents fun challenges for you to conquer. The most important fact to remember about your mental skills is that they are *under your control*. Although you cannot control how a game is officiated and how another team or opponent plays, you can control how you react to the game and practice situations that you encounter. This means you can still get enjoyment from playing in games when your team loses. You—not the spectators, opponents, or officials—are in control of how much fun you have.

> You can practice mental skills during travel to and from games, during team practices, and on your own.

Another essential realization concerning basketball mental skills is that you can practice them almost anywhere and anytime. They may be developed on or off the court. For example, an excellent time to practice mental skills is during the travel to and from games. Practicing mental skills during this "down time" allows you to use your travel time more constructively. Once you have learned some of the key mental skills and training aspects presented in this book, you can usually practice your mental skills without the assistance of another player or

coach. Although one of the exciting elements of a team sport like basketball is the development of teamwork, it is also fun to be able to work on some skills on your own. Just as it can be enjoyable to practice your dribble, jump shot, or moves to the hoop by yourself, working on the necessary mental skills individually can be a lot of fun. That is what this book is about: "*FUN*damental" basketball.

> *You should never try to be better than anyone else, but never cease to be the best you can be.*
>
> —John Wooden (Former UCLA, men's basketball coach and Hall of Famer who has won more NCAA championships—10—than any other coach)

> *I look for players with multidimensional games . . . players who push themselves to be the best they can be.*
>
> —Pat Summitt, head basketball coach of the University of Tennessee, who has led her teams to six NCAA national championships and coached her 1997–98 team to a perfect 39-0 record. Coach Summitt also led the United States Olympic women's basketball team to the Gold Medal in 1984.)

*FUN*damental Points to Remember

1. To be a complete basketball player or coach, you must practice both mental and physical basketball skills.

2. Mental skills (i.e., concentration, confidence, handling pressure) may be improved with proper practice.

3. Mental skills are *under your control*.

4. Improving mental skills is *FUN*damental.

FUNDAMENTAL SKILLS OF THE COMPLETE BASKETBALL PLAYER

SCOUTING REPORT -CHAPTER TWO-

You will read how to

1. Use imagery, concentration training, and self-talk to improve as a complete basketball player or coach.

2. Use a Mental Practice Notebook to improve your mental basketball abilities.

3. Use a sense of humor to keep coaching or playing basketball fun.

*FUN*damental Skill #1— Mental Practice

I visualized where I wanted to be, what kind of player I wanted to become. I knew exactly where I wanted to go, and I focused on getting there.

—Michael Jordan (NCAA, Olympic, and 6-time NBA champion)

Imagine the following scenario. You are playing on your home court while your team has the ball and is down by one point with 10 seconds left to play in the overtime period of the championship game. Your teammate has the ball at the top of the key as the clock is ticking down the final few seconds. The

> *Feel the ball. See the clock. Hear the crowd.*

crowd is on their feet yelling and screaming for a victory. Your opponent is guarding you "like a glove" on the right side of the lane, about five feet from the basket. You give a strong head-and-shoulder fake toward the basket, then quickly move out to the right of the free throw line and circle about 16 feet from the basket. Seemingly all in one motion, you receive the basketball, make a quick pivot, and shoot a jump shot. You can see and feel the ball leave your hand with a slight counterclockwise rotation as it flows through the air. The ball enters the basket —"nothing but net"—as the final horn sounds. Your teammates and fans surround you at the center of the court

> Your imagination can inspire you to improve your game.

cheering their approval. You are the hero! This is just an exercise in imagination for you right now, but we will show you how this sort of mental practice can help you to be more successful and enjoy these types of clutch situations.

Anyone who has played or coached basketball has imagined a similar situation or pretended to be in this situation on a home or playground basketball court. Our imaginations can be

a source of inspiration to continue to improve our basketball skills for game situations just like these. However, we can employ an important psychological skill that can be more effective than our imaginations, a skill known as *mental imagery*. Imagery is a form of mental practice where you visualize yourself performing basketball and psychological skills the way you would ideally like to perform on the court. One of the greatest centers of all time, Bill Russell of the Boston Celtics, studied his opponents so he could "play movies in his mind" to be better prepared for the games.

What is mental imagery? It's more than just seeing yourself playing basketball. Many players use more of their senses than just seeing themselves perform while using imagery. For example, many athletes report being able to *feel* the ball in their hands and their movements on the court, as well as *hear* crowd noise, ball dribbling, and basketball shoes squeaking while going through an imagery session. Thus, many athletes report using more than one of their senses to make the imagery session more realistic. It is important that you use this skill in the manner that seems to be most effective for you. That means that if you can only visualize or see yourself or you can only feel the movements while imaging, imagery practice can still be effective for you. Let's take a look at how you can use imagery to achieve basketball success.

Understanding Mental Practice

The mental approach to things is what separates players at every level.

—Lisa Leslie (Western Conference starter in the 2000 WNBA All-Star Game, first-ever WNBA All-Star Game MVP, member of the 1997 All-WNBA First Team, and member of the 1996 USA Women's Olympic team that won the Gold Medal)

Mental toughness is to the physical as four is to one.

—Coach Bob Knight

The first thing you need to do to get started with imagery is to understand how and why imagery can be an effective practice technique. When you practice a physical skill such as dribbling a basketball, it helps you to become more familiar with the skill.

Your goal is to be able to dribble without having to look at the ball or having to think about the mechanics of dribbling. The more you practice dribbling, generally the more confident you become and the better you become at practicing this *FUN*-damental skill. Imagery is another form of practice that can

> Imagery allows you to become familiar with a new skill by practicing it in your mind.

help you in a manner similar to physical practice. If you mentally practice dribbling the ball correctly, you will become more confident and more familiar with the skill. As you can see, mental practice can help you improve just as physical practice can. However, mental practice has one big advantage: You can mentally practice any skill almost anywhere and anytime.

Getting Started

To begin practicing imagery, it is probably best to go somewhere where you can practice without being distracted or disturbed. As you grow more acquainted with imagery, you should be able to practice it just about anywhere.

Get into a comfortable position that you can maintain for about 15 minutes. We recommend that you sit with your back up against a wall and your legs placed uncrossed, straight out in front of you. Again, as you grow more proficient at imagery, the position will not be as important. Then, close your eyes and begin to take some deep breaths. The goal of the first part of the imagery session is to try to become relaxed.

Once you begin to feel relaxed, try to image yourself performing a psychological or physical skill. You could image yourself playing defense, making a bounce pass, or shooting a layup. Try to incorporate as many of your senses as possible. *See* yourself performing, *feel* the ball in your hand, *hear* the ball bounce and the squeaks of the basketball shoes on the floor. Also, *feel* the sweat on your forehead, *hear* the crowd, and *feel* all eyes on you. As stated earlier, you should mentally practice in the way that works best for you. For example, if you cannot hear basketball sounds while mentally practicing, do not be discouraged. You may develop this skill later on as you practice more. It is NOT a requirement to incorporate all of the senses in order for imagery to be effective. It is more important that you simply MENTALLY PRACTICE.

When You Should Practice

We recommend that you incorporate mental practice into your everyday practice routine. Mental practice may be done be-

> Try to mentally practice once a day, 3-5 times a week for about 15–20 minutes.

fore, during, or after your physical practices or games. You can decide what works best for you. At the very least, aim to mentally practice once a day, 3–5 times a week, for about 15–20 minutes per session. In the beginning you may set an intermediate goal of practicing for about 10 minutes until you become comfortable with the technique. The more often you practice, the quicker you will become a better imager, which should lead to reaping the benefits of mental practice much sooner. As you become more involved, you may desire to practice more than once a day.

A good way to begin your imagery practice is to write down a weekly schedule of when you can consistently practice im-

PRACTICING IMAGERY

■ Find a place where you won't be disturbed.

■ Assume a comfortable position you can hold for 15 minutes.

■ Try to relax by closing your eyes and breathing deeply.

■ Imagine yourself successfully performing a psychological or physical skill.

■ Incorporate as many senses as possible—sight, sound, smell, touch.

agery. If possible, try to select the same time every day or evening. This makes it more likely for you to remember to practice. For example, schedule a 15-minute session every morning at 7:00 a.m. during the school year, or, if it is more convenient for you, schedule an imagery session every night at 9:00 p.m. It is important that you schedule a time that you are most likely to stick to. It is a great idea to create a weekly chart to record the days and time periods that you mentally practice. You could also use your own rating system (1 = *needs much improvement* to 5 = *excellent*) to score how you think the imagery practice went that day. Your imagery chart may look something like the following:

My Mental Practice Schedule
Sunday . . . . 9–9:10 pm 3
Monday . . . . 9–9:12 pm 3
Tuesday . . . . 9–9:15 pm 4
Wednesday . . . . . . 9–9:15 pm 4
Thursday . . . . Skipped . . . . . . Too much homework
Friday . . . . 9–9:18 pm 5
Saturday . . . . 9–9:21 pm 4
Week Total Practice Time = 6 days, 1 hour and 31 minutes
Average Weekly Session Rating = 3.83

Mental Practice Notebook

By keeping a record of your practice time and evaluating the imagery sessions, you can keep track of your progress. You may even want to keep more detailed information concerning your sessions, such as what you mentally practiced in each session and/or specifics about what you were able to do or not do during a particular practice session. We call this a Mental Practice Notebook (MPN). In your MPN, you may also want keep records of your "mental performance" at games and practices. For example, an entry in your MPN may resemble this:

February 12

Our team won a big conference game tonight. Although I scored less than normal, I played consistently good defense. My concentration was outstanding, and my gem talk (see page 30 for an explanation of gem talk) was good. I played as a highly confident player tonight and remembered to do imagery before I shot most of my free throws.

Mental Skills Scores

(MSS: 1 = *needs much improvement* to 5 = *excellent*)

Concentration = 5

Gem talk = 4

Confidence = 5

Imagery = 4

Overall MSS = 4.5

By recording and evaluating your mental skills performance in this manner, you have a good method of tracking your mental strengths and areas for improvement. These records can be used like game statistics to help you see the mental skills you need to work on and notice the skills that are successfully working for you.

IMAGERY FAQ'S

■ Should I imagine myself from a viewer's perspective or my own?

■ What if my imagery doesn't happen as I planned?

■ Do I have to believe in imagery for it to help me?

Frequently Asked Questions About Imagery

Viewpoint. "Sometimes I see myself dribbling the basketball as if I were watching myself from the bleachers. Is this OK?" At this moment, close your eyes and imagine yourself shooting a short jump shot. Did you image yourself from a spectator's point of view, or did you see yourself shooting from your own "shooting" perspective? Either method can be effective. Use what is more comfortable and works for you. If you find your-self using only one of these viewpoints, try the other just for fun. You may find that being able to use either viewpoint gives you more variety in your mental practice. Perhaps you will de-cide to use a combination of these viewpoints during your practice sessions. If you find you are unable to use one of the viewpoints, don't worry that your imagery skills are lacking. Everyone has different strengths. It is important that you prac-tice with the viewpoint you are comfortable with.

Control. "Sometimes when I practice imagery I find that my imagery doesn't happen as I planned it—why?" For example, you may wish to imagine making 10 shots at a spot on the court 12 feet from the basket, yet when you mentally practice this, you find that you miss 3 of the shots. Don't be alarmed. This is a common occurrence. This imagery situation may in-dicate an area of your game in which you are weak, and it's a good sign that you need to practice that part of your game more. Usually this type of situation can be overcome with more mental and physical practice.

Belief. "Do I have to believe imagery will work for it to help me?" One of the most important aspects of imagery and men-tal practice is the belief that it will be effective. You must be-lieve it will work for you. Your attitude toward imagery is criti-cal in its ability to have an effect on your game and personal improvement. If you believe imagery will work, you are more likely to consistently practice. The more you practice, the more imagery has a chance to help you.

> *I have used visualization techniques for as long as I can remember. . . .*
> *It wasn't until later that I realized it is something most players have*
> *to learn. . . . The process of seeing success before it happened put me*
> *in a positive frame of mind and prepared me to play the game.*
>
> —Michael Jordan (Considered to be one of the greatest all-around players in the history of basketball, written in his book, *For the Love of the Game*)

Using Imagery During Games or Practice

Once you become a skilled imager, you can use imagery before, during, or after a game or practice. In many of these instances, you may image for only a few seconds to get yourself ready to perform. For example, just before going out to play a game, you can take a few moments to imagine yourself shooting, passing,

> Use positive imagery to gain confidence seconds before you perform.

and being ready to play. In this manner imagery serves as a pregame preparation technique. During a time-out in the second half of a game, you may quickly image the inbounds play the coach has just instructed you to run. In this instance, imagery helps you to mentally perform a skill only seconds before you actually do it and gives you confidence. After the game you may "run a play through your mind" that did not go the way you wanted it to. In this manner imagery can serve as your "mental video" to review your performance after the contest is over.

The key point to remember here is that imagery is not only a practice technique, but also a performance technique. Almost all of the great basketball players have implemented mental imagery to their distinct advantage. Imagery can play a key on-court role during your practice and game situations.

I'm daydreaming about hitting a winning shot. I remember I was so calm, so relaxed. . . . I envisioned being a hero in a game. I saw myself hitting the game-winning shot. . . .
—Michael Jordan remembering his visions before the 1982 NCAA championship game in which he made the championship-winning shot

*FUN*damental Skill #2—Concentration Awareness and Training

I think fear sometimes comes from a lack of focus or concentration.
—Michael Jordan

Basketball is a fast-paced sport that demands much physical and mental talent. One of the constant challenges of playing good basketball is to maintain your concentration and to focus on the right elements at the proper time. There are many events in playing basketball that may lead you to lose your focus (i.e., feeling pressure, crowd behavior, "trash" talking). How many times have you been told that you need to "focus" or "concentrate" better? Has anyone ever told you *specifically* how to concentrate better? One vital psychological skill is to know

> Learning how to concentrate will help you maintain focus.

how to regain focus on the correct elements during practice or a game. You may physically practice basketball for numerous hours to prepare yourself to perform well at game time. However, if you lack proper focus, you are likely to be disappointed with your performance during "prime time." Before you can acquire this skill, you must have a way to think about concentration that allows you to control how and where you focus.

Understanding Concentration

As you begin reading this sentence, follow these directions. Without looking, notice where your right foot is located right now. Next, pay attention to how your stomach moves as you breath. By doing these things, you are actually controlling your concentration. In other words, you are controlling what you are able to focus on. Being able to control, direct, and maintain the proper concentration at the appropriate time is crucial to being successful in basketball. In order to be able to change your focus, you must understand how this skill operates. You must be able to think about the skill of concentration in a way that allows you to know what it is *specifically* you are trying to focus on.

The Specifics of Concentration

Think of concentration as having *many* or *few* things to focus on. This means you can choose to try to focus on numerous things during a basketball game (your game strategy, your follow-through on your shot, the opponents, rim, ball, etc.), or you may decide to focus only on one or two of these. Also, think of concentration being focused inside or outside of you.

You can focus on your own thoughts and feelings (e.g., I'm nervous, my heart is beating fast), or you can focus on items in the basketball environment (lights, nets, backboards, scoreboard, fans, etc.). These concentration options may be combined to form four possible ways to concentrate while playing basketball. Remember, all great athletes have the ability to concentrate and shut other things out of their minds.

Four Ways to Focus

With an **MO** (many-outside) focus, your focus is centered outward or away from yourself, and you are observing many things. Basketball players using this focus are usually *assessing* the court situation. In other words, before deciding what offensive play to call out for the team to run, a basketball player will see who is on the court, look at the defense, and check the time on the game clock. In this way, the player is evaluating the situation.

The focus labeled **MI** (many-inside) means you are thinking about the basketball situation. You may be running through many different ideas, pictures, or scenarios in your mind in order to try to come up with the right solution or answer to meet the game situation. In this framework of concentration, your focus is centered inward and considering many factors.

If you focus within the **FI** (few-inside) framework, then you are thinking about only a couple of things and your focus is inward. It is in this focus that players mentally *prepare* and may begin thinking about one or two aspects of their upcoming performance or use imagery to get themselves ready. However, the **FI** focus may also be the focus of concentration players are in when they *choke*. In this scenario, you may begin to think negative thoughts such as "I am so nervous" or "What if I commit a turnover that messes up my team's chance to win?" These are not the types of thoughts that lead to successful game or practice performances.

Finally, the **FO** (few-outside) focus is usually the appropriate focus basketball athletes need to be in while shooting, passing, and catching the ball. For example, when you are shooting a jump shot, at the moment you are releasing the ball toward the basket, you need to be concentrating only on the rim or spot on the backboard you are aiming for (FO focus). Thinking of other things will be a distraction and therefore cause you to miss or—worse—shoot an air ball. Another example may be used in rebounding. Once you get into your proper "boxing-out" position, your focus should be solely on the ball.

If you take time to really consider these frameworks of concentration in this way, you will soon figure out that each type of focus may be helpful to your performance. The key to concentration is knowing and being able to quickly change the appropriate focus of concentration at the proper time. Your first step in being able to do this is to remember these four frameworks. (Refer to the following diagram for examples of how each focus may be used.) This will give you a way to think about your concentration skills that will help you to be able to change focus as the basketball situation requires.

Concentration = Three Pointers:
Three Important Aspects of Concentration

One pointer. A basketball player should not attempt to be in two of the four concentration frameworks simultaneously. This simply means that your performance will be hurt if you try to be in two different focuses (e.g., MO and FI) at the same time. This is usually very difficult, if not almost impossible, to do.

Two pointer. You probably have a certain focus of the four frameworks that you rely on the most. We all have a particular "preference" of concentration that we feel most comfortable with or are simply better in. Therefore, we spend most of our time in this preference. When we are nervous or pressured, we usually resort to this concentration framework. Being too nervous is usually a hindrance to being able to concentrate properly, which results in a loss of concentration flexibility. Errors in performance occur when your focus does not match the basketball demands. In other words, if a skill requires you to focus (FO) on the basketball (e.g., catching a bounce pass) but you are assessing (MO) the positions of the defensive players while the pass is coming toward you, you are likely to fum-

FOUR BASKETBALL CONCENTRATION FOCUSES

Many-Outside

Observation of the entire court situation (teammates, opponents, ball location, etc.)

Few-Outside

Concentration only on the rim while releasing the ball for a shot

Many-Inside

Trying to decide which of several plays to call on offense

Few-Inside

Using imagery at the free throw line before shooting

ble or muff the pass, causing a turnover. Another example of how the wrong focus at the wrong time can cause an error may occur at the free throw line. If, *while* releasing the basketball on the attempt, you are thinking about the defense to be run *after* the shot, you will be more likely to miss the free throw. You should focus on the rim *while* shooting and then focus on your defensive position *after* the attempt.

Three pointer. Concentration flexibility is the key to most basketball performances. You need to be able to *switch* focus as the situation requires. Many players can switch, but do so either too fast or too slowly. This causes errors, because they are thinking ahead or thinking in the past. Also, you may be in the wrong focus for what you are doing at a particular time. You should spend most of your time in the here and now—the present. However, successful players are those who can maintain their concentration flexibility and switch into the proper focus as the basketball situation demands.

Helpful Concentration Tips

Full-court concentration. This style of concentration occurs when a basketball player tries to maintain complete, intense concentration from the beginning to the end of the game or practice. The advantage of this style is that by not taking any mental concentration breaks, you do not have to worry about regaining concentration. An example of this style would be

CONCENTRATION POINTERS

- Maintain one concentration focus at a time.
- Find the focus framework that works best for you.
- Learn to switch from one focus to another as needed.
- Practice concentrating both on and off the court.

players who. once they walk into the gymnasium, begin to concentrate, and keep concentrating until they leave the gym for the day. The major disadvantage of this style is that maintaining concentration for long periods of time, without any breaks, is mentally tiresome. Therefore, you may risk losing concentration sooner than you want to and leave exhausted.

Concentration with many time-outs (TOs). With this concentration strategy, you concentrate but "free the mind" with several concentration time-outs during stoppages in the practice or game. For example, during a game, you stay focused while the clock is running. Yet after a stoppage in play, you joke with the referees or simply hum your favorite song. The purpose of this strategy is to allow the mind to concentrate for longer periods of time by giving the mind mental breaks in between. The disadvantage of this strategy is that you run the risk of having trouble regaining concentration after the time-outs. To regain your concentration, you need to use a "cue word" (see self-talk in the next section), like "ready" or "focus." to get your mind back on the action.

Concentration with few TOs. This concentration mode is used by hoopsters who maintain concentration while taking only a few mental time-outs. For example, you may take a mental break only during time-outs or at the end of a quarter or half. In this method you have fewer concentration time-outs and run less risk of having trouble regaining concentration, while hopefully being able to maintain concentration for a longer period.

Again, you will probably find that one of these three styles matches your normal style of concentration. However, it is important to realize that what may work for you during one performance may not seem to work during another. When this occurs, you need to find the style that will help you to maintain your concentration for the longest period. Finding a consistent concentration style is important to helping you become a better player. However, it is important to be *flexible* if your normal style is not working on a particular day.

Concentration Practice

Now that you are aware of the various modes of concentration, you should devote some time to practicing concentration skills both on and off the basketball court. Like physical skills, concentration is a skill that must be practiced in order to improve. One of the best ways to practice concentration on the court is to make sure during basketball practice that you concentrate appropriately. It helps also if the practice sessions sometimes simulate the real game conditions. That way you can practice concentration in conditions that closely resemble your game-day situation.

However, many basketball players find that some "off-the-court" concentration exercises are helpful in enhancing their concentration abilities. An excellent way to practice concentration is to use imagery exercises. Any time you are perform-

> Focusing on images and senses while practicing imagery will also improve your concentration.

ing mental imagery you are actually conducting another form of concentration practice. Mental imagery requires you to be *focused* on your images and senses. Imagery allows you to practice all of the concentration components discussed earlier. Imagery is a highly recommended technique because, if you so desire, you can work on at least two skills at the same time—good physical performance and good concentration.

You will also want to try to create in your imagery the same emotions experienced while at basketball practice or during a game. Some people feel that always getting relaxed before performing imagery will help you to become more relaxed during an actual performance. However, it is probably unrealistic to believe that basketball players can be as relaxed on the court as they would be during an imagery session. Imagery is probably more effective if it is treated and performed as a *"mental simulation"* of possible, realistic, basketball performance events. Try to image yourself performing psychological skills successfully, too. Image yourself being confident, controlling your temper, and staying focused while shooting, dribbling, and playing defense. For example, let's say that you have been given the challenging assignment of guarding the leading scorer of the opposing team. To meet this challenge successfully, you will need to remain active, energetic, and focused. Hence the night before and the day of the game, you should image guarding the opponent while experiencing (during the imagery session) the anxious energy and necessary level of concentration to do your job.

Another form of concentration practice is relaxation training. To foster good relaxation, you must be focused on reducing your stress. This requires you to concentrate. Techniques such as deep, slowed breathing require skilled concentration

> Your concentration will improve as you learn to relax. Breathe slowly and deeply as you reflect upon peaceful scenes.

for a certain amount of time. Also, you may picture scenes in your life that give you peace (e.g., lying on a float in a swimming pool) and reflect upon them. Becoming relaxed requires you to stay focused on what you are doing while not allowing yourself to be distracted, so by practicing relaxation skills, you can again foster two good skills simultaneously—controlling your stress level and enhancing your concentration.

A basketball concentration "off the court" exercise that can be fun and easy to practice is one that allows you to specifically practice the FO focus of attention. To do this drill, you need to go to a quiet area where you will not be disturbed. (When you become skilled at this drill, you will be able to practice it almost anywhere, even in noisy environments.) Next, get into a comfortable position. You should be in a position that you can maintain for 5 to 10 minutes at a time with minimum movement. Then, hold in your hands or place in front of you a basketball. If a basketball is not available, then you can visualize the ball, rim, or backboard. Next, you should try to focus on the ball or image while saying or thinking of an "assist word" or short phrase such as "ball," "rim," "board," or "focus." Use an assist word that has meaning for you. In other words, when you notice that your mind begins to wander from the task at hand, simply say "on the ball" or "focus," or any assist word (or short phrase) that you chose, to get you back into the proper concentration mode. Your goal is to try to focus on the ball or thought while repeatedly saying or thinking your assist word. If outside thoughts or other distractions come into your mind, do not fight them. Simply let these thoughts come

> Remain calm as you concentrate; it becomes more difficult if you try to force it.

and go. This will allow you to get rid of them quicker and keep a focused, calm attitude during your exercise. By practicing with a calm attitude, you improve your ablty to calmly focus your concentration without having to force concentration when you are actually performing. This can be crucial, because *usually when you try to force yourself to concentrate, it only makes it more difficult to do so.* By practicing with an assist word or short phrase, you should be able to use this assist word or phrase during actual performance to help you regain your concentration quickly.

It is recommended that you try this exercise twice a day for at least 5 minutes each time. As you get better at this exercise, you may find that you can go longer than 5 minutes. BE

PATIENT, though. This will take work. Being able to do this exercise for 5 minutes, dealing effectively with potentially distracting thoughts, is quite an accomplishment.

Understanding concentration is the first step in learning how to control your concentration abilities to play better basketball more of the time. By spending time practicing your concentration skills both on and off the basketball court, you will enhance these important psychological skills.

Concentration is the supreme art. . . . The masters all have the ability to discipline themselves to eliminate everything except what they are trying to accomplish.

—Dale Brown (Former Louisiana State University men's basketball coach who took his LSU teams to two NCAA Final Fours; college coach of Shaquille O'Neal)

*FUN*damental Skill #3— Positive Self-Talk (Gem Talk)

Negative thoughts will produce negative results.

—Dale Brown

Unfortunately, in today's game some basketball players devote a great deal of time, energy, and preparation to "trash talking" with an opponent. Trash talk (see chapter 6) has become a "game within the game" for some players in which they try to verbally "psych out" each other or get others off their game. For example, while a player shoots, the trash-talking defender may state, "You're gonna miss." Yet there is a type of talk that is much more important and crucial to your performance—

Replace trash talk with self-talk.

positive self-talk (or *gem talk*; notice this is spelled "g-e-m" talk rather than "g-y-m" talk). The reason we call positive self-talk gem talk is that it can be a "treasure" and the "rock" foundation for your basketball performance. Self-talk is simply the thoughts you think or say to yourself. The reason self-talk is so important is that what you think about yourself or your situation will determine your attitude, confidence, and emotions in *every* situation. In other words, no matter how hard you work physically to prepare for a game, if you lack the confidence necessary to handle the situation, your performance will suffer. The neat thing to realize about self-talk is that you are in control of it. You can control how and what you think about yourself, another player, or a situation. It is crucial to performance that your self-talk be POSITIVE self-talk.

Many times basketball players are critical of their own performance. They are hard on themselves. Some basketball players will say and think negative things to themselves to try to improve or motivate themselves. For example, let's say that a point guard attempts to make a "skip" pass from the right wing to the left wing. But a defensive player steals the ball and scoots in for an easy layup. The guard might have thoughts such as "That was a dumb pass!" or "Why did I try that?" These types of negative thoughts might continue long enough to cause the point guard to make more mistakes, which would, in turn, lead to more negative thoughts. Negative thinking of this sort is a mistake, one that many players and coaches have made. If you do it over and over, negative thinking (or negative self-talk) becomes a habit. Habits don't just happen; they are learned with much practice. Any habit that was learned CAN be changed, or unlearned.

Changing Thought Habits

Many of us have bad habits we would like to change (like biting our fingernails). Once you realize this type of negative thinking is a bad habit, you have made the initial step to changing it. You probably don't even realize how often you think negative thoughts about yourself. To give yourself an idea of how often you have thoughts that can be detrimental to performance, try this simple exercise. While playing your next pickup game, wear a rubber band around the wrist of your nondominant hand (the one you shoot with the least). Each time you think something negative about yourself, pull the rubber band back and slightly pop it against your wrist, just enough to make it sting a little. For example, let's say you go in for an easy, uncontested layup, but the ball rolls off the rim and is rebounded by your opponent. You may think, or even yell loudly, to yourself something like "I just blew an easy shot!" If you do,

> Thinking negative thoughts is like committing a foul against yourself.

pop your wrist with the rubber band. After the game, think back to how many times you had a negative thought and had to pull the rubber band—or notice how red your wrist is! You will probably be surprised at how often you say or think "foul" things to yourself. It is important to view negative thinking as committing a "foul" against yourself. Your goal is to reduce your fouls, so you can mentally stay in the game.

Once you realize how much of a habit negative thinking has become, it is time to take steps to create a more positive thinking habit (gem talk). It is a good strategy to write down some of the common "foul" statements you say or think about yourself. On a sheet of paper or a computer, create two columns. Make the left column the "foul" statements, and label the right column the "rebound" statements. In the left column, record some of the negative statements you have used. Beside each statement, in the "rebound" column, record a more positive, realistic, and confidence-producing thought you plan to use the next time. The "rebound" statements will be your gem-talk statements (positive self-talk). A good way to do this is to think of what *you would say to a teammate* who had just committed the same mistake you made. You normally may tell a teammate something like "That's OK" or "Don't worry about it. Keep shooting, the shots will fall." In other words, your goal is to *be your own best teammate or coach*. Typically, these statements may be future oriented. Instead of even mentioning or focusing on the mistake just made, say or think what you should do the *next time* you are in that situation. For example, your record may look something like this:

Self-Talk Statements

FOULS	REBOUNDS
1. I just blew an easy layup!	**1.** I will make that layup the next time.
2. S/he has scored on me three times in a row! I'm hopeless.	**2.** I will try to play her/him even closer on the next attempt.
3. That was stupid! Why did I try to make that pass?	**3.** I will give a better fake before I throw that pass the next time.
4. I can't guard him/her. S/he is too good.	**4.** I'll do the best I can and make him/her work harder.
5. This game is over. Our team stinks.	**5.** I'll just keep playing hard to find a way to contribute to this game. It's not over yet!

After completing your list of "fouls" and "rebounds," the next step is get more "rebounds" than "fouls" in your next contest. In other words, after you make a mistake, instead of using a "foul" statement or thought, say a "rebound" statement to yourself. To do this, you have to first stop the negative thoughts. This is more difficult than it sounds. If you have ever tried to break a bad habit, you know how tough this can be. Thought habits seem to happen so quickly they seem like automatic thoughts over which we have no control. Remember that YOU DO have control over your thoughts. You want to create new thought habits to substitute for the "foul" thought habits. One of the best ways to stop those negative thoughts is to say or think "STOP" to yourself when you feel the unwanted thought coming on. Some players visualize a stop sign (like on a street or road) to block the thought. After you interrupt the negative thought or statement, substitute a "rebound" statement in its

place. By continuing to do this, soon you will create more optimistic talk, which should have a positive impact on your performance. These are usually the type of encouraging statements that you would say to a teammate.

Why Not Say or Think Rebound Statements to Yourself?

Aim to be your own best teammate or coach. Remember that
everyone makes mistakes, even Shaquille O'Neal, Pat Summitt,
John Stockton, and Lisa Leslie; the successful basketball players and coaches are those who learn to recover the most quickly
from their mistakes.

Using a Sense of Humor

One of the best tactics you may use in your gem talk is to have a
sense of humor with yourself. Being able to grin or laugh at yourself (especially after making mistakes) can be very helpful in
"keeping your chin up" and taking off some of the pressure that
you may put on yourself. Many players react to a poor performance with a temper tantrum or some outward show of disgust as
a way to show their teammates or coaches that they do care
about their performance. However, there are many other, positive, ways to show others that you care about your performance,
such as giving a good effort at practice, taking extra time to work
on your game, or saying something to cheer up a teammate.
Keep in mind that after you make a mistake, no matter what you
say to yourself or how big a temper tantrum you may throw, *it
will not erase the mistake.* So why put yourself (and sometimes
the team) through more anguish by torturing yourself with negative thoughts or a tantrum? You may as well try to find some
humor in the situation. As mentioned earlier, you have probably
said some humorous words to teammates in order to cheer them
up. You can say similar statements to yourself to keep yourself in
a more positive state of mind. If you can make using a sense of
humor a thought habit, you will find that playing basketball will
be even more enjoyable for you and those around you.

*Do not permit the things over which you have no control to adversely
affect the things over which you should have control.*
—Coach John Wooden

*FUN*damental Points to Remember

1. Imagery is a form of mental practice where you visualize yourself performing physical and psychological basketball skills the way you would ideally like to perform on the court.

2. Mental practice can help you improve, just like physical practice.

3. Incorporate mental practice into your everyday practice routine.

4. Mental practice may be done before, during, or after your physical practices or games.

5. Begin and keep a Mental Practice Notebook.

6. Be aware of four types of concentration: many-outside, many-inside, few-outside, and few-inside.

7. The key to concentration is recognizing and being able to quickly change the appropriate focus of concentration at the proper time.

8. We all have a particular "preference" of concentration that we feel most comfortable with or perform better in.

9. Know the three styles of concentration: full-court concentration, concentration with many TOs, and concentration with few TOs.

10. Self-talk is what you think about yourself or your situation. It will determine your attitude, confidence, and emotions in *every* situation.

11. Use your sense of humor to keep basketball fun.

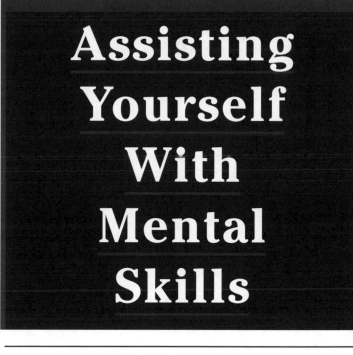

Assisting Yourself With Mental Skills

SECTION II

3

SHOOTING

How to Lessen "Basket Interference"

One of the keys to becoming a good shooter is the ability to focus totally on the basketball goal or backboard while shooting, blocking out other thoughts. Most players who go into shooting slumps or are "cold" become that way not because of the defense played on them by an opponent, but because they "play defense on themselves." They mentally block their own shots while shooting by thinking such thoughts as "I hope I don't miss this one" or "I really don't want to shoot this shot." The three *FUN*damental skills can be used to prevent this from happening.

SCOUTING REPORT -CHAPTER THREE-

You will read how to

1. Use the *FUN*damental skills to become a better shooter.
2. Use an imagery scenario to practice shooting.
3. Develop a consistent mental and physical routine to improve free throws.

Imagery Practice for Shooting

If you remember the points on mental practice discussed in chapter 2, imagery can be a great way to practice shooting from different positions and angles on the court, and under many different circumstances. At one time or another, most basketball players dream of making the last shot of the game for their

> Use imagery as a warm-up or a post-game review.

team to win the game. Imagery is a more productive way to practice those situations (and others) regularly without having to be on, or even near, a basketball court.

Imagery should be a part of your practice regimen. It can also be used as a warm-up before the game or as a review after the game. Before a game, you can imagine the type of defense you need to play and practice making the bounce pass into the post player. After the game, you can run certain plays through your mind to reinforce what you did right on those plays or to correct what you did wrong. You can use imagery at the gym or at home almost every night, and it must be used consistently. Let's say you wish to work on shooting 3-pointers from near the top of the 3-point arc, near each wing, and from each side near the baseline. With imagery, you can mentally practice shooting in many different situations, from being in a gym by yourself to shooting in a championship game in front of a "packed" arena! You simply play the "video in your mind" over and over again. For example, let's say you wish to practice a game-like situation. Here is an imagery scenario that you could use.

You are on offense positioned at the free throw line-extended, behind the 3-point line on the right side of the rim. You notice the defense is laying off of you. You wave your arms in the air to get your teammate's attention. You feel yourself wanting the ball. The teammate sees you, then throws the ball toward you. You see the skip pass coming across court to you from the other wing. As the ball comes toward you, you position yourself to be ready to take the shot. You see and feel the ball come into your hands. Once you have caught the ball, you square your shoulders toward the goal and quickly "eye" the basket. While totally focused on the rim, you raise your arms above your head, bend your knees, and begin to release the ball toward the basket. You sense a defender is coming toward you, but you remain focused on the basket. You feel the ball leave your hands as you perform a perfect follow-through, and see the flight of the ball as it takes a slight arc toward the goal. The shot felt good as it left your hands, and you feel confident the shot is going in. Then, the ball swishes through the basket, barely moving the net. The referee raises both hands to signal a successful 3-point goal, and you feel exhilaration from making the shot as you hustle to get into position to play defense.

Again, only your own imagination limits what you may practice with imagery. With consistent mental practice sessions like this, imagery can not only help you develop your shooting ability, but it also can help you develop confidence in your shot and give you the proper focus while performing.

Concentration and Gem-Talk Keys for Shooting

The mental key to being a successful scorer is to be able to be in the proper frame of focus once you have decided to take the shot. It is important that once you decide to shoot, your concentration be focused solely on the rim or backboard (if you plan to bank in the shot). The frame of reference, as discussed

> Avoid distracting thoughts when you shoot. Focus only on your target.

in the concentration chapter, is the "few-outside" (FO) focus. It is important that while you are looking at the goal, you are not thinking distracting thoughts such as "I hope I don't miss this," "I've missed three in a row," or "Maybe I should pass instead." These types of distracting thoughts represent the "few-inside" (FI) focus, which can interfere with your shooting. Just before and at the point of release of your shot, your focus should be ONLY on your target. One way to help you stay in the FO frame of reference is to use self-talk. Decide for yourself an assist word that you want to use while shooting and focusing on your target. Use a word that means something to you and is simple to use (typically a one- or two-syllable word) and that will help you focus on the goal. Examples of some appropriate self-talk assist words may be "rim," "ring," "basket," "focus," or "smooth." Then, while physically and mentally practicing your shot, think the assist word as you take your shot. This mental technique will help you to be in the right focus and keep you from thinking other negative thoughts that may serve to distract you from making the shot. Until you get back into your shooting groove, you will probably have to remind yourself to do this. However, you will eventually make it an automatic process that will not require a constant self-reminder.

Mental Routine for Shooting Free Throws

The crazy thing is that the foul line is the one place in the basketball game where you can be completely selfish and still help your team.

—Rick Barry (Second-best free throw shooter (90%) in NBA history, who shot his free throws underhanded)

Most good coaches will tell you to develop a physical routine for shooting each free throw. For example, this means that every time you go to the charity stripe, you could dribble the ball three times, place the ball in the same "shot pocket," look at the basket or the middle of the hole, take a deep breath, then shoot the free throw and maintain the follow-through until the shot is over. The purpose of developing a physical

> Develop a physical routine that you repeat every time you shoot a free throw.

routine is to make each free throw, no matter what or where the situation is, more similar and familiar. This means that

shooting a free throw in a gym all by yourself would be performed exactly the same way as if you were shooting crucial
free throws in a double-overtime play-off game. This encour-
ages using the correct and successful techniques *every time*.

Most coaches and players have found that having a physical
routine is beneficial, and therefore, almost every basketball
player uses the same physical shooting routine before every

free throw. This being the case, the question has to come to mind, *"Why isn't every player a good free throw shooter?"* The answer lies in the *mental routine*. Although almost all players use the same physical routine, there is much inconsistency in their mental approach to shooting free throws. A free throw is the only shot in basketball that is exactly the same every time. It is only the situations in which the free throws are taken that vary greatly. Some players are better free throw shooters during the early part of a game, but their percentage goes down in the final, critical seconds of a close game. Other players focus better when more is "on the line," such as in the last few minutes of a hard-fought game, but have trouble during the first half, when the free throws are seen as less important. To get basketball players to focus as they should from the charity stripe at any time during a game, players must have one consistent mental routine to use for all game situations. The best free throw shooter in NBA history (90.6%), Mark Price, said

---

Your mental free-throw routine can include

- visualizing an image of the ball leaving your hand and going into the basket.
- repeating your assist word to yourself.
- counting as you dribble before each shot.
- taking a deep breath before shooting.

---

something to the effect of, My free throws are always the same. I get the ball from the officials, I take three dribbles and shoot it. As I release the ball, I say, 'Heel to toe,' to myself, to remind me to go up on my toes. Although players on a team may develop various different mental and physical routines, it is important that you find a routine that works especially for you.

Let us share with you an example of a mental routine that uses all three of the *FUN*damental skills. As you are waiting to receive the basketball from the official and after you have positioned your feet properly at the free throw line, you could quickly image (eyes open or closed) the ball leaving your hand

and entering the basket. This "quick imagery" is a confidence booster that will help you focus on your upcoming throw. After using imagery, focus on the ring and be sure to think your assist word, such as "ring" or "hole," repeatedly. Repeating your assist word will help you to get mentally focused. As you prepare to actually receive the ball from the official, you could think "ready" or "calm." (Remember that it is important to choose an assist word that is meaningful and will work for you.) This will help you to remain composed as you begin your routine.

After you get the ball, we recommend you count as you perform the dribbles before each free throw. In other words, if you dribble the ball three times before each free throw, then as you take the first dribble think, "one"; as you take the second dribble, think "two"; and as you take the third dribble, think "three." This counting again serves as a focusing technique. More important, however, counting to yourself will stop you from distracting yourself with negative thoughts (e.g., "I hope I don't choke this time"). Then, as you look at the rim and take a deep breath (a deep breath will help you to relax), think "calm" or "relax." This will again keep you from becoming too nervous or excited just before you shoot. Next, begin to focus on the rim and think the word "rim" or "ring." This will put you in the FO concentration focus (see chapter 2) that is necessary to perform the free throws successfully. Pick something to look at like the front or back of the rim. Then, as you think "rim" or "ring," shoot the free throw. Also, if at times you have difficulty maintaining your follow-through, you could think "form" or "through" after you release the ball. Following is a summary of this mental free throw routine. Of course, you can and *should* adapt this routine so that it becomes comfortable and confident for *you*.

Notice that your mental routine keeps you focused on shooting each free throw. This stops you from distracting yourself by worrying about making or missing the shot. You are focused on the process of shooting, rather than its outcome. Many basketball players unnerve themselves at the line because they are so focused on making the shot or "choking" on the free throw line.

Obviously, it is important that you devote much practice time to becoming a good free throw shooter. As you perform your physical routine, use your own mental routine with it. It is important while practicing free throws that you practice both

Mental and Physical Free Throw Shooting Routine

PHYSICAL STEP	MENTAL STEP
1. Get positioned at line.	1. Use quick imagery and/or think "rim" or "hole."
2. Wait for ball.	2. Think "relax" or "calm."
3. Receive ball and dribble.	3. Count each dribble.
4. Take a deep breath.	4. Think "relax" or "calm."
5. Stare at the rim and shoot.	5. Think "rim" or "hole."
6. Maintain follow-through.	6. Think "through" or "form."

your physical and mental routines so both routines will become a habit or "second nature" to you. Soon you will be able to perform the entire free throw routine automatically, without having to make yourself think about each part of the routines. This will help you to develop an overall consistent free throw shooting routine that will help you to be a good, consistent, and "clutch" free throw shooter.

I've never really understood why more players don't make the effort to become good free throw shooters. It just takes practice and hard work. And concentration.
—Larry Bird

*FUN*damental Points to Remember

1. Consistent mental practice can help you develop confidence and give you the proper focus while shooting.

2. Use an assist word (e.g., rim, ring, basket, focus, or smooth) while shooting and focusing on goal or backboard.

3. Find a consistent mental and physical routine (that works especially for you) to use at the free throw line.

4

PLAYING DEFENSE

Using Mental Skills to Improve Defense

Many basketball players spend countless hours thinking about and practicing their offensive skills. One reason for this is that you can practice offensive skills by yourself. All you need is a ball and a hoop to work on your jump shot or dribbling maneuvers. Often this leads to neglect of or too little emphasis on playing defense.

Although you can work on some physical aspects of playing defense by yourself (e.g., footwork), usually you need at least another player

SCOUTING REPORT -CHAPTER FOUR-

You will read how to

1. Use imagery and concentration skills to become a better individual and defensive team player.
2. Use gem talk to keep your focus while playing defense.
3. Maintain your confidence while playing defense.

present to help you sharpen your defensive abilities. However, imagery is an excellent way to work on your defensive skills without anyone else being there with you.

> Practice defense alone by using imagery.

Team Defense

Mentally practicing your defensive moves, position, and confidence can be just the lift you need to assist your teammates in playing overall good team defense. Coaches will tell you that if four of the five players on the court are playing defense, this is usually not enough to be effective. In other words, team defense means *everyone* on the court must be actively involved. To be a part of a strong defensive team, you need to actively practice your defense. One way to do this, once you have learned your team's various defensive schemes, is to mentally practice your responsibilities. For example, if you are the guard near the top of the key on a 1-3-1 zone, you may practice where you should be positioned with each movement of the ball and the opposing team's players. As you imagine the ball being moved around the court, you can visualize yourself moving to the correct position. You can even image yourself deflecting or intercepting a pass. For example, you imagine yourself playing at the back (nearest to the basket) of a 1-3-1 zone defense. You

Maintaining Concentration While Playing Defense

- Concentrate on the ball and the opposing players.
- Use gem talk to stay alert.
- Use cue words to focus on certain aspects of your game.

see the offensive team set up in a 2-3 offense. The ball is passed to the guard on your right side. You see your teammates collapse on the player with the ball. You visualize the guard jumping into the air to make a desperation pass across the lane to your left. However, you see yourself anticipate this, run to cover the passing lane, and intercept the ball.

While actually playing defense in practice or a game, it is important to keep focused on the appropriate game events to be effective within your team defense. Maintaining your concentration on the opposing players and the ball will allow you to better anticipate your next defensive reaction to your opponent's move. A good way to keep yourself focused while playing team defense is to use gem talk to remind yourself to stay alert and single cue words to help focus on the key aspects of your defensive game. For example, if you are one of the defensive guards near the free throw line on a 2-3 zone while the ball is passed into the middle of the lane, you could say, "Collapse" to remind yourself to move down and help defend the player with the ball. Then, if the ball is passed back out to an offensive player on your side of the key near the 3-point line, you could think "face" to remind yourself to get your hands in the face of the potential shooter; or as the ball is being passed on the other side of the court, you can remind yourself to stay between the player and the ball by thinking "player-ball." Knowing where to be and what to do on team defense is a key to being a more confident and effective defensive team player.

1-on-1 Defense

Defensive mental imagery may be the key you need to become your team's "stopper." By using imagery, you can learn to better anticipate what the opposing players may do to get by you or get a shot off over you. Sometimes you will be playing against players' tendencies (e.g., likes to go right, will shoot the midrange jumper) you are aware of. Maybe you have seen them play, have played against them several times before, or have received a good scouting report. However you have learned about them, you can prepare specifically for this particular defensive assignment. In these situations, a good sug-

Use imagery to anticipate and react to other players' moves.

gestion is to visualize what you need to do to stop or slow down their moves. For example, if you know that a player you will be guarding likes to give a ball fake before most shots, then you can mentally practice not going for the fake and being ready to get your hands up for the potential shot.

If you don't know much about the player you will be guarding, you can still use imagery to practice the footwork and hand movements necessary to play tough one-on-one defense. This may be especially helpful right before a game or at half-time. Let's say you will be guarding a good left-handed shooter who likes to give a head fake, shoulder fake left, then go right, stop "on a dime," and shoot a midrange jump shot. You could use imagery to imagine yourself not going for the head fake, playing more on the right side, staying close to your opponent, and jumping up when he or she shoots, getting a hand in the face. At the very least, this will help you to get in the correct "mind-frame" and prepare you to play good defense. As mentioned earlier (chapter 2), you may practice imagery both as a part of your normal basketball practice routine and before or during a game. The key fact to remember to become a better defensive player is to spend extra time working on your defensive skills both physically and mentally. Mentally practicing your defense and knowing how to be, and stay, mentally ready to play defense can go a long way to improving your overall game.

Using Self-Talk to Improve Defense

As with team defense, self-talk will help you prepare to play on-on-one defense. Whether you are playing against a player you know a lot about or an unfamiliar opponent, use a few cue words to keep you aware of your defensive duties. The cue words will vary depending upon whom you are playing against.

Keep yourself confident with positive self-talk.

You may tell yourself "left," meaning the player likes to drive to the left side, or you may remind yourself to have "quick feet" to better stay up with the offensive player. You may also say general things like "stay balanced" or "stay grounded" to remind yourself not to jump until the shooter does. Self-talk will help to remind you of your opponent's tendencies while you are in the defensive stance and will keep you focused on what you are supposed to do.

However, one of the most important duties of self-talk is to keep you confident as a defensive player. The best way to be able to do this is to *consistently* practice (mentally and physically) your defensive skills. Another way to do this to remain a *confident* defensive player. The way to keep your confidence is to think confident thoughts about your defensive skills, especially after you have been beaten on defense. It is easy to be confident after blocking a shot or stealing the ball from your opponent. The great defenders are able to remain confident even after they have allowed someone to score on them. No matter how good a defensive player you are, there are going to be times when your opponents will score over or around you. It is important to remember that the most you can ask from yourself is to play the best defense you know how. You must think thoughts that will keep your defensive efforts up and not allow you to become discouraged.

Consider this example. A player gives a head fake, then drives past you for an easy layup. You become frustrated and mad at yourself because you feel embarrassed at letting the team down. While you continue to feel upset, the player gets by you again. Now you are so mad you can't think clearly. This type of negative self-talk reaction will cause you to lose your defensive focus and make you a liability on defense. However, you can control how you react to a defensive miscue. Once the player gets by you, you could think, "I'll not let that happen again," "I'll stop that move next time," or "I learned from that mistake." Rather than pity yourself or feel embarrassed, you can encourage yourself to give the best effort possible. Remind yourself that your teammates know that you work hard on defense, and everybody loses a defensive assignment occasionally. With this more optimistic gem talk, one defensive miscue is less likely to lead to another.

Thinking realistic but positive thoughts will help keep you in the game defensively. For example, if you are 5'10" tall and you get caught on a switch guarding a 6'8" player, you probably shouldn't think, "I'm going to block this shot." A more realistic thought is "I'm going to try to distract this player by putting my hands in the air." This type of positive, practical thinking will help you to keep from growing discouraged and to do the best you can in all types of defensive situations. As we stated in chapter 2, it is very important to remember that *YOU are in control of your confidence*!

*FUN*damental Points to Remember

1. Use mental imagery to practice both your individual and team defensive skills.

2. Maintaining your concentration on the opposing players and the ball will allow you to better anticipate your next defensive reaction to your opponent's move.

3. A good way to keep yourself focused while playing team defense is to use gem talk to remind yourself to stay alert and use cue words (i.e., face, collapse) to focus on the key aspects of your defensive game.

4. The great defenders are able to remain confident even after they have allowed someone to score on them.

5. Thinking realistic but positive thoughts will help keep you in the game defensively.

5

BECOMING A BETTER ALL-AROUND PLAYER

I was aware of my success, but I never stopped trying to get better.

—Michael Jordan (5-time NBA Most Valuable Player, 9-time NBA All-Defensive First Team, 10-time NBA scoring leader, and 13-time NBA All-Star)

SCOUTING REPORT -CHAPTER FIVE-

You will read how to

1. Use the *FUN*damental skills to become a more complete, all-around basketball player.
2. Get out of and deal with a slump.
3. Add diversity to your game, such as improving your "off hand" more quickly.

Skill Improvement

One aspect that all great basketball players share is their willingness to try new things in order to improve. This attitude is how they have made themselves stand out above the rest. All levels of basketball players can improve some aspect of their game.

One goal that all basketball players should strive for is to become the best all-around players they can be. This means you should attempt to improve *all* aspects of your game. For example, if you are a good jump shooter, but weak at the free throw line, then you should practice your free throws. However, becoming an all-around player also means that you have good mental skills, can play good team and individual defense, dribble, shoot, pass, rebound, and have variety to all your game skills. It is obvious that to become an all-around player, you need to be above average at numerous basketball skills. The *FUN*damental skills (mental practice, concentration, and self-talk) can help you to achieve all-around proficiency.

Imagery. Imagery can be very helpful in assisting you to improve any physical and/or psychological skill (see chapter 2). Therefore, one way to improve any basketball skill is to use a consistent mental practice of that skill. For example, let's say you're already a good dribbler; nevertheless, you want to improve your crossover dribble. Then, by all means possible, you should practice the crossover every time you have a basketball in your possession; yet for those times when you don't have a basketball or court to practice on, use imagery to see and feel yourself skillfully executing a crossover dribble. For example, you imagine a defender playing your right side because you are dribbling with the right hand. The defender is in a crouched position with both hands up. You visualize yourself making a sharp shoulder fake to the right, then feel your right hand quickly pushing the basketball ahead and to the left side of your body. You get by the defender, who is now back on the heels, for an easy layup. In this example, you are improving a skill that you possess while adding another dimension to your game.

However, if your goal is to become an all-around player, you will need to practice as many skills as possible at almost every

> All great basketball players are willing to try new things to improve.

practice session. We know that it is practically impossible to rehearse every basketball skill every day. This is where imagery can really come in handy. For instance, your coach may spend

most of practice time one day on teaching a new offense against a 1-2-2 zone. However, you feel you really need to work on grabbing rebounds and throwing outlet passes. Once practice is over, you may not have a teammate who is able to stay at the gym with you to help you work on outlet passes. With imagery, you can do this in "the videotape in your mind" by visualizing your outlet passes while sitting alone in a room. Other days, you may simply be too fatigued to physically practice some of the necessary skills. Fortunately, mental practice requires very little energy to perform the following scenario. You visualize yourself positioned about eight feet from the basket when an opponent shoots a jump shot from the right side. You move toward a position about three feet from the left

> Even when you have very little energy, you can still practice imagery.

side of the rim. You imagine feeling the body contact as you "spread out" to block out the nearest opposing rebounder. With your arms now extending toward the ceiling, you jump up to grab the rebound with both hands, remaining focused on the ball. After you secure the ball, you look to the wing where you anticipate a teammate to be waiting for the outlet pass. You use a baseball throw to lead the teammate, who is making progress up court. You feel the ball leave your hand, and it feels like a good pass. The pass is crisp and right on the mark. Your teammate catches the ball and continues up court on the fast break.

Concentration. Because you are now aware of ways to appropriately concentrate (chapter 2), you can use ways to maintain your concentration longer and/or more effectively. For example, if you find that you have trouble concentrating for entire

> Feel free to adopt different concentration styles on different days.

games or practices, you can change your style of concentration. Remember that one concentration style may work for you one day, whereas another may work on another day. You may discover that one concentration mode is good for one type of practice, whereas another works better for a different skill. Your goal is to be able to find the right concentration style (i.e., full-court concentration, concentration with many TOs, or concentration with few TOs) each day in order to perform the best at your practices and games. This will help you to be more effective at improving your skills, which will lead to your becoming a better all-around player.

Self-talk. Positive self-talk is important in becoming the all-around player that you want to become. It is important to stay motivated to improve in as many basketball areas as possible. One way to stay motivated is to remind yourself how enjoyable it is to improve ("I love to get better!"). If you are very competitive, remind yourself that your opponents may be practicing while you aren't ("I wonder how hard my opponents are working today"). The thoughts you allow yourself to think will be an important force in whether or not you put in the time to improve.

Skill Correction and Slumps

Many basketball players who get into a slump will helplessly wait until the slump ends on its own. One of the best ways to handle a slump is to *actively* attempt to get out of it. Remember this statement: "When in a *slump*, work to get over the *hump*."

Instead of waiting for the slump to end by itself, it is usually best to spend extra mental and physical practice time to overcome this temporary state.

> Instead of giving into a slump, use imagery and concentration to get out of it.

There will always be times when a skill you know you can normally perform will not work for you for a game, a day, or even longer. For example, you may know you are a consistent shooter from about 15 to 18 feet. However, one day while practicing you find that your jump shot will not fall. In times like these, you have to analyze what you have been doing on a particular skill in order to improve it. If a coach, teammate, or relative can videotape you while in this shooting slump, that can be a big help, and if you have an earlier videotape of when you were shooting well, this can help you to get back into the shooting groove. By comparing your slump shooting with your good shooting, you may be able to detect obvious mistakes such as a lack of follow-through or not having your shoulders "square" to the basket. Imagery is very helpful for correcting this. You can use imagery to visualize correcting the mistakes that are causing you to miss. After a bad shooting day, use an imagery session to correct what seems to be going wrong. For instance, you may notice that you seem to be leaning to the right as you go up to shoot. You can then use imagery to correct your balance during the jump shot. Imagine going up for your jump shot. Feel the ball release with perfect form, and hear the "swish" as it goes through the net. Do this six or seven times until you feel confident again.

Concentration can also be a big problem for players when they go into a shooting slump. Often, players will find that if their shots are off, they are inappropriately thinking about something else (i.e., many-inside focus or few-inside focus— see chapter 2). Although they should be focusing on the rim or backboard, they are worrying about how the coach is going to react, or they are being distracted by the defenders. If this happens to you, remind yourself that at the moment you are about to release the shot, the focus should be on the rim or backboard ONLY (few-outside focus). Again, the use of an appropriate self-talk cue word (e.g., "rim" or "hole") can be helpful in this scenario. Being aware of the different ways to concentrate and how to control your concentration will help you to make these corrections more quickly.

Using the "Off" Hand

One of the most important physical basketball skills a player can learn is to be able to shoot, pass, catch, rebound, and play defense with the off hand. The off hand is the nondominant hand. If you are right-handed, then it is your left hand. If you

are left-handed, then the off hand is your right hand. If a defensive player knows you are going to shoot or dribble only with the right hand, this awareness will allow the defender to "cheat" toward the right hand. If an offensive player knows that a defensive player will use only the right hand to block a shot, then the offensive player can use that knowledge to an advantage to "get off" a shot or draw a foul.

It is important that you use your encouraging self-talk to tell yourself how important it is to be adept with the off hand. See it not only as a way to add variety to your game to make you less predictable to opponents, but also as a skill that will take some time to develop. A good way to learn how to use your off hand is while you are dribbling, shooting, passing, and playing "d" with your dominant hand, to pay close attention to how the dominant hand moves. By doing this, you will know better how to do these same movements with the nondominant hand. You will also need to be aware of the actions of the other hand. Here is an example of a way to do this for learning to shoot a layup or "baby hook shoots" with the nondominant hand.

For a right-handed player, stand near a basketball goal, take one or two steps, and shoot a few layups with the right hand (dominant hand). Each time you do this, pay close attention to foot, arm, and hand movements that are necessary to execute

> Before you practice with your nondominant hand, imagine yourself executing the movement successfully.

the layups. Notice how you step toward the goal, cup the ball, and jump, as well as how you use the other hand, then use imagery to feel and see yourself executing these movements with the dominant hand. Once you feel good about imagining these movements, use imagery to see and feel yourself executing these skills with the nondominant hand. Once you feel ready, try to mirror these movements by actually shooting a layup with the left hand (nondominant hand). Keep working on the off-handed layups until you feel comfortable with them. Notice how your other hand is used to keep your balance or hold the ball. You can then practice the same technique for shooting off-handed jump shots beginning with short distances and moving to longer

Cue Words and Phrases to Help With Off-Hand Use

step

balance

eyes on the basket

smooth

follow through

control

wrist

wave 'bye to the ball

form

distances—even shooting free throws this way. This technique may be used to learn to dribble, play defense, pass, etc. with the nondominant hand. Be patient, though. It will take practice—physical and mental practice. Remember to use imagery sessions, in addition to your physical practice, to help learn these new skills with the off hand. For example, imagine yourself using a crossover dribble with the off hand to get past the defender or throwing a bounce pass to your teammate. Imagery can help you to feel more comfortable and make these newer skills "second nature" to you. Here are some cue words that good basketball players use to help them learn to shoot with the off hand. Look at the list and choose one or two words or phrases to use: step, balance, eyes on the basket, smooth, follow through, control, wrist, wave 'bye to the ball, and form. By focusing appropriately, staying positive, and using physical and mental practice, you will be able to add valuable diversity to your game. This diversity will help you to reach your goal of becoming a better all-around player.

*FUN*damental Points to Remember

1. Use imagery to practice all mental and physical skills to become a better all-around player.

2. "When in a *slump*, work to get over the *hump*." Instead of waiting for the slump to end by itself, it is usually best to spend extra mental (i.e., imagery) and physical practice time to overcome this temporary state.

3. One of the most important physical basketball skills a player can learn is to be able to shoot, pass, catch, rebound, and play defense with the off hand.

4. By focusing appropriately, staying positive, and using physical and mental practice, you will be able to add valuable diversity to your basketball skills.

SPORTING BEHAVIOR: BEING A GOOD "SPORT"

Sportsmanship, the players' insistence on their rights and observance of the rights of others. It is playing the game vigorously, observing the rules definitely, accepting defeat gracefully, and winning courteously.
—James Naismith (The inventor of basketball)

SCOUTING REPORT -CHAPTER SIX-

You will read how to

1. Show good sporting behavior— be a "good sport."

2. Appropriately deal with "psyche out" attempts (i.e., trash talking).

3. Use the "three-seconds rule" to your advantage.

Being a Good Sport

Showing good sporting behavior (the new term for sportsmanship) is a goal that many coaches, parents, and players often stress. Many participants, in all sports, feel that this may be the most important behavior athletes should learn and embrace. Unfortunately, some of today's players do not exhibit appropriate sporting behaviors. Although it has always been a violation of the rules to act inappropriately, unsporting behavior has become so common that the governing bodies of the various levels of basketball have written rules that specifically prohibit this bad behavior. The rules stipulate that players, coaches, bench personnel, and team followers (including fans) are not to disrespectfully address officials/referees or use obscene, vulgar, or inappropriate language or gestures; and they are prohibited from taunting or baiting an opponent. Why these types of bad behaviors have increased is not the focus of this book. However, there *are* ways to learn to make good sporting behaviors a habit, which makes basketball more enjoyable for all.

Trash Talking

One aspect of the sport of basketball that has become more commonplace at all levels of play is "trash talking" or "talking junk." Sometimes this "talking" is called the "game within the game." Many times, the goal of trash talking is to get the opponents off their game. Some players do it to humiliate the opponent. These behaviors have become so commonplace that often after a great play, opponents misunderstand an honest celebration as an action to belittle them. Trash talk can lead to rough, physical play; verbal abuse; and actual fights. Obviously, these actions do not belong in the sport of basketball and are violations of the rules. You can alert the coach to this illegal behavior and let the officials take care of these occurrences by calling the appropriate fouls. The officials will appreciate this action on your part.

Many times, however, officials are unable to prevent trash talking. One way to keep yourself from getting caught up in a

Remember that trash-talkers just want to break your concentration.

trash-talk "war" with opponents is to remind yourself of the main reason your opponents are trash talking to you: *Their goal*

is to get and keep your mind away from what you are supposed to be doing. There are several wrong ways to respond to trash talking. Players often respond to trash talk by trying to show the other person up. Only a few very good players can respond this way. The majority of players end up trying too hard. By trying too hard, you may take shots that are not within the flow of the offense or are not part of your normal game, or you may try to steal the ball or block a shot only to find yourself in foul trouble very quickly. If you respond this way, then the trash talker has won, has "psyched you out." Other players "back down" from trash talkers. They become timid and don't try hard enough. They give less effort than is normal. If this occurs, then trash talkers have also achieved their goals and caused you to play poorly.

Some players respond to trash talk by attacking their opponents with their own trash talk. Again, few players can ably respond this way and still play up to their potential. What usually happens here is that players become so concerned with what to "say" or "come back" with next that they fail to stick with their game or the team's game plan. The trash talkers have won again by psyching out the opponents, taking their minds off the appropriate game duties.

So what is the best way to respond to trash talking? The most effective way to respond to trash talk is to block it out by using your excellent concentration skills and to play within your own abilities. This is not easy to do, but the three *FUN*damental skills will be very helpful in keeping you from being psyched out by an opponent's trash talk. With imagery, you can mentally practice an upcoming opponent's using trash talk against you. In these sessions, imagine hearing the taunts but ignoring them and playing your normal game. In imagery sessions and in actual on-court situations, it will be helpful to have some cue words or phrases to use. For example, if players from the opposing team begin to trash talk, think, "I know

HOW TO DEAL WITH TRASH TALK

■ Use your concentration skills to block it out.

■ Imagine ignoring an opponent's trash talk during your imagery sessions.

■ Think cue words or phrases to remain calm.

■ Control your focus.

what they're trying to do. It's not going to work on me" or think words like "calm" or "cool" to help you remain calm.

Another way to combat trash talk is to concentrate on task-focused (i.e., few-inside or few-outside) thoughts. Be aware of and control your focus. This means that when the other players begin talking, remind yourself of what you are supposed to do (e.g., run the offense, keep your feet moving, block out, focus on the rim, watch the ball). If you can respond this way when opponents begin trash talking, then their trash talk serves only to help you play better. You can use this trash talking to remind you to focus. If you respond this way, you win! They will expend so much energy trying unsuccessfully to distract you that they will play worse. Using the *FUN*damental skills can enable you to deal with trash talking in a sporting and more effective manner.

Special Trash-Talk Practice

Another way to practice playing against trash-talking players is through simulations. In other words, you may play a trash-talking game with your teammates. While playing against your teammates, have them use trash talk against you, the same way that an opponent would. REMEMBER NOT TO GET CARRIED AWAY, THOUGH! You and your teammates must always be aware that the real purpose of trying this exercise is to help you deal with trash talk appropriately, not to upset or humiliate anyone. If this exercise is done with the right mindset, it can be a fun way to help you to learn to deal more easily with trash talk.

Psych-Out Attempt

Another way that an opposing player may try to psyche you out is by giving you a compliment. Many players who are aware of this tactic sometimes still allow themselves to be tricked. This tactic attempts to change your concentration focus, usually from few-outside to few-inside or many-inside. Here is an example of how this works. You have just made three jump shots in a row over the same defender. After you make the third shot and begin heading down court to set up for defense, the defender goes by you and says, "Great shooting. You really have a nice follow-through." You may react to this on your next shot attempt by paying closer attention to your follow-through. Remember, at the point of releasing the shot, your focus should usually be on the rim or backboard (see chapter 3). Now, at the point of release, by focusing on your follow-through, you allow the defender to change your shot concentration focus, which sometimes leads to your missing the shot. Again, the defender

> Don't allow compliments to ruin your concentration.

was able to do this by giving you an apparent compliment. Sometimes an opponent may simply say, "You are really hot today!" Again, the goal of the opponent is to get you thinking about "why" you are hot, thereby changing your focus from what has been working for you. It is important to be aware of this tactic so you will remember to use the appropriate self-talk or assist words to avoid falling prey to another psych-out strategy. If you find that you have fallen for this sneaky tactic, use an assist word or phrase (e.g., "ball," "rim," "time to refocus") to get your mind back on the proper focus.

Emotional Control

Chapter 2 discussed how to use gem talk to make playing basketball more enjoyable. Remember that the reason self-talk is so vital to emotional control is that what you think about yourself or the situation will determine your attitude, confidence, and emotions in every situation. You are in control of your own emotions. Emotions can make the sport of basketball even more fun and exciting. However, remaining in control of your emotions is the key. Losing control of your emotions may cause a variety of basketball performance problems, including inferior play, fouls, fighting, ejection from one or more games, or injury. Therefore, it is important that you develop positive thought habits or "rebound" thoughts (see chapter 2) to help you maintain control of your emotions. Again, the three *FUN-*

damental skills can help with this. Imagery sessions may be tailored to visualize game situations not going the way you desire; then, you mentally practice staying in emotional control. For example, you image yourself committing a turnover. Then,

Imagery and self-talk can help you keep your emotions in check.

instead of getting upset, you picture yourself staying calm and focused. You can develop self-talk to help you stay in control. Words like "calm," "cool," "stay even," or positive self-statements like "That's all right" and "I'll make up for it" can help you remain focused on the task at hand.

The Three-Seconds Rule

One way to keep in control of your emotions and not experience serious "out-of-control" outbursts is to avoid letting your emotions build up. Some players will try to hold in their emotions but eventually will blow up, which leads to an embarrassing situation. A way to prevent this is to use the "three-seconds rule."

When things go wrong, rather than holding emotions in only to explode later, you can give yourself *just three seconds* to say or think positive or negative thoughts to yourself. You can be critical, yell at yourself, or say something more positive, but you must limit yourself to three seconds. (You will find that much can be said in three seconds!) After the three-second time limit is up, you must begin to focus on what you are supposed to do next. This technique allows you to "let off steam" and then get focused for the next situation. It helps prevent the major explosion that occurs from trying to hold your emotions in. By limiting the time of your emotional outbursts, it keeps you from having prolonged emotional ups and downs. By adhering to the time limit, you also help yourself get quickly refocused on the appropriate game tasks. The three-seconds rule can be a helpful method of remaining in control of your emotions. Just be careful that if your team needs you to respond immediately, you save your three seconds for a moment in the game or practice when you have time to pause.

*FUN*damental Points to Remember

1. Many participants, in all sports, feel that good sporting behavior may be the most important behavior athletes should learn and embrace.

2. The main reason opponents use trash talking is to get and keep your mind away from what you are supposed to be doing.

3. Use the three *FUN*damental skills to help you deal with trash talking appropriately.

4. Remember that compliments from opponents may serve as psyche-out attempts.

5. Emotions can make the sport of basketball even more fun and exciting. You are in control of your own emotions!

6. Use the three-seconds rule. Give yourself *just three seconds* to say or think positive or constructive thoughts to yourself before focusing on what you are supposed to do next.

7

DEALING WITH REFEREES, FANS, OPPONENTS, INJURIES, AND OTHER SITUATIONS

SCOUTING REPORT
-CHAPTER SEVEN-

You will read how to

1. More completely understand the role of basketball officials (referees) to make you a better basketball player or coach.
2. Appropriately handle on- and off-court distractions.
3. Keep a healthy balance between basketball and the other important areas in your life.

Officials

Basketball officials (commonly called "referees") are an important part of the "team" within an organized basketball game. Basketball officials are there to insure the game is played by the intention of the rules. Although some players, coaches, and spectators see these persons as "necessary evils," this could not be further from the truth. Basketball officials are a *necessity*. Could you imagine a high school, college, or professional game played without the referees? There would surely be so many disruptions due to arguing that it would be difficult to complete most games. Basketball referees insure that games are played within the spirit of the rules, with as much fair play and equality as possible, for all players.

Although most basketball aficionados somewhere deep down in their psyches realize that this is true, some participants forget this in the heat of the game. Players, coaches, and spectators often blame the officials for the team's

> Basketball referees are members of an officiating team and play an important role in keeping competition fair.

poor play or even losses. If players and coaches really believe that officials cause losses, then players and coaches should give credit to the officials when the team wins. Have you ever heard a coach or player give credit to an official for helping them to win a game? Probably not. Unfortunately, this blaming type of attitude is unhealthy and irresponsible. The fact of the matter is honestly and simply this: Players and coaches—not officials—win or lose basketball games. Players and coaches make many more mistakes (e.g., turnovers, missed shots and free throws, lack of preparation) during a game than officials do.

One of the best ways to keep yourself from being upset or bothered by calls that you disagree with is to understand what the actual role of the basketball official is. Few people are willing to take on the task of officiating a basketball game. Many view basketball officiating as one of the most difficult officiating/umpiring tasks in all of sports. One of the best ways to see how difficult it is to ref a game is to try it yourself.

This may give you a better appreciation of what these individuals experience. If you are not willing to do this, consider some of the following points about basketball officials. Most basketball officials enjoy refereeing because they have a true interest in and enthusiasm for the game. They also find the task challenging and exciting. (These are the same reasons that players and coaches get involved.) Also, officials physically and mentally train. Officials study the rules book. Just as you and your teammates work together during a game to play your best, the crew of officials is also a team on the court attempting to do their best. Just as you will make mistakes during a game, so will the officials. The major difference that you must remember about officials is that (unlike players, coaches, and spectators) referees are not concerned with who wins or loses a game. This allows officials to call a game in a fair, objective, and unbiased manner.

By understanding more thoroughly the role of the basketball official, you can help yourself to stay better focused on your game. If you can tell yourself that you have a job to do and so do the officials, you should be so consumed with your game responsibilities that you don't have time to be concerned with the officials. You can also remind yourself that arguing with officials almost never changes the call. Therefore, getting upset or arguing with an official is usually just a waste of your energy. However, there will be times when you will disagree with an official's call. It is helpful to have cue words (e.g., "That's OK," "It all evens out," or "They are doing their best") to say to help you keep calm and get focused on your game. As with other basketball skills, you may use imagery to practice these thoughts. You can visualize a call going against you, but see yourself able to stay calm and quickly focus on what you need to do next. Once you use your cue words to keep yourself calm, remind yourself to get focused on the next task. For example, if a foul has just been called on you and the opponent will be going to the charity stripe, you might say to yourself, "That's OK. Now I need to box out along the free throw lane." In this example, use your self-talk to calm yourself down and then control your concentration by focusing on the next immediate task.

Opposing Fans

Remember the word *fan* is a shortened version of the word *fanatic*. There are opposing-team followers who will try to disrupt your play with their taunts and yelling in order to help their team win. There are two ways to deal with these types of

spectators. First, you can treat opposing fans' verbal jabs the same way you can treat opposing players' trash talk (see chapter 6). Remind yourself that the opposing team's fans are trying to *get and keep your mind away from what you are supposed to be doing.* They are trying to get you off your game. Again, use imagery, cue words, and concentration focus to keep yourself focused on the task at hand. Remember that fans' being on your back is a compliment to your ability. If you show discipline by not reacting to them, they will usually become mum.

Reframing allows you to imagine any crowd is cheering for you.

Another way to deal with boos, hisses, silence, or yelling from the opposing fans is to "reframe" them. Some basketball players pretend that opposing fans' actions are meant to inspire them to play better. So when they hear a fan yelling at them, they use their self-talk, saying, "The more they yell, the better I'm going to play." They may reframe the "silence" of the opposing team's crowd as a "cheer" for them. Reframing can allow you to acquire motivation or inspiration from almost any spectator situation.

Off-the-Court Situations

Things turn out for the best for those who make the best of the way things turn out.

—John Wooden (Hall of Famer who coached his UCLA teams to 10 NCAA national championships)

Although the sport of basketball may be important to you, there are many areas of life (e.g., family, school, work, and social life) besides basketball. You should always remind yourself that, although you are involved in basketball, basketball is only one part of your life. It is important to keep a healthy balance between playing basketball and the other areas in your life. Sometimes these outside areas may have an effect on your basketball performance. Although they may sometimes hinder your basketball performance, your goal should be to try to limit this as much as possible. One way to do this is to try to think only about basketball during your basketball practice or games. This is easier to do at some times than it is at others. For exam-

> Clear your mind of everything but basketball during games and practices.

ple, let's say you had a big argument with your good friend. You then go to basketball practice thinking about the argument, what you wished you had or had not said, and how you are going to remedy the situation. You continue to consider this during the entire practice. Obviously, you probably do not have a worthwhile basketball practice. Remember: While you are at basketball practice, you can do little or nothing to handle the argument with your friend. Therefore, there is no need to let it interfere with your practice. Use your self-talk to remind yourself that while you are at practice, you should think and play only basketball. Use cue words to focus your concentration appropriately. For example, say to yourself, "Basketball now, problem later" to tell yourself that you will deal with the argument after practice. This method of dealing with outside distractions from basketball can be used for numerous situations such as receiving a bad grade in a class or worrying about a sick relative.

Teammates and Coaches

No matter how enjoyable the sport of basketball is, there will be some other players (possibly teammates) and coaches whom you may not like or be able to get along with. Although basketball can be more fun when everyone likes everyone else, the team or coaching staff does not have to suffer because of a few less-than-close relationships. One way to deal with this is to use your self-talk to tell yourself that you are going to make the most of the situation. It is important to stress to yourself THE TEAM FIRST. In other words, although it may not be easy at times, you should try to consider the team's needs above your own personal dislikes. Even if you do not have a good relationship with one of the coaches, remember that the coach is usually trying to help you and the team improve. Sometimes talking about how you feel with a teammate can help you deal with this. Remind yourself of the following statement, especially if you and the teammate(s) are vying for the same position: Their effort should cause you to work harder, which makes the overall team a stronger unit.

Injury and Rehabilitation

One of the most nagging and aggravating situations you can encounter in basketball is to become injured and have to recover. Recovery from injury requires both mental and physical rehabilitation. Your attitude toward the injury and rehabilitation process will have a significant impact on your recovery.

> The way you think about your injury has a huge impact on your recovery.

One of the best strategies to deal with this situation is to view the injury and recovery process as another challenge to be faced in basketball. Just as you have formidable opponents to play against, consider your recovery from an injury as an opponent to be dealt with. The *FUN*damental skills can be helpful in the mental and physical rehabilitation of your injury.

Imagery can be a valuable technique during times of injury. Imagery can be used for two important purposes. First, during the time when you are not allowed to physically practice basketball, imagery allows you to mentally practice your skills. Although it cannot take the place of physical practice, imagery may help you not to be so rusty when you return to play. At the very least, it can help you to stay involved with the team. For instance, if a coach introduces a new defense while you are injured, you can visualize your movements on this new defense so it will be easier for you to catch on when you return to actual playing time. Also, it can be very motivational for you during rehabilitation to image yourself playing basketball again, because that is the purpose of rehabilitation. It may also help you to be less apprehensive about reinjury. Here is an example of an imagery session you could use to keep you motivated while recovering from a knee injury:

Mental Rehabilitation Imagery Scenario

See yourself practicing in the gym by yourself. You are casually dribbling the basketball from one sideline of the court to the other. The basket is on your left. You feel the ball touch your hand on each dribble. You can hear the squeaking of your shoes on the wood floor and the ball hitting the floor on each dribble. You dribble to one sideline with the right hand, then back to the other sideline with the left hand. You then begin to pick up speed, working in some behind-the-back, through-the-legs, and crossover dribbles. Your knee feels strong and flexible. Then, as you approach the top of the key, you make a quick drive toward the left side of the basket. You plant your right foot on the ground near the goal, jump up with the ball in your left hand while aiming for a specific spot on the backboard, and bank the ball into the goal. You feel confident that your mental and physical rehabilitation has been successful.

Another way that imagery may help during the rehabilitation process is by speeding up the recovery. Some athletes have reported using imagery to visualize their injury getting better. For example, if you have a pulled muscle, you could use imagery sessions to visualize your muscle healing. You could get a picture from a book or the Internet of what the

---

While you're injured you can use imagery to

- mentally practice your skills.
- visualize yourself performing new playing strategies.
- visualize your recovery.

muscle looks like (or imagine what it looks like). Then imagine the spot on the muscle that is injured as a gray area. Let the color blue represent the healing process. Next, visualize a small section of the gray area slowly turning blue and progressing until the entire gray area has turned blue. This type of healing imagery could be done every day before or after (or even during) physical rehabilitation. At the very least, using "healing" imagery may help you to have more of a feeling of control over your recovery process. In other words, healing imagery gives you another positive way to meet the challenge of recovery and rehabilitation.

How to Have Fun When You're Way Behind or Way Ahead

Playing in a close basketball game is usually exciting. Players and coaches typically do not experience difficulty staying mentally in the game in these contests. Unfortunately, there will be times when your team will be ahead or behind by a large number of points. Contests where you feel the game is over, although there is much time left on the game clock, can sometimes make it easy to lose your focus. The best way to handle being either ahead or behind is to use your self-talk to remind yourself of your team and individual goals. Even if you feel the winner of the game has (for all practical purposes) been decided, there are usually some game goals that can still be accomplished. Perhaps your team set a rebounding goal that has not been reached. Maybe a team goal was to keep the opposing team from scoring over a certain number of points. It is possible that you have a personal goal of giving 100% effort (playing or cheering the team) or showing good sporting behavior regardless of the game situations. All of these are examples of worthwhile individual and team goals that help you to focus and keep your intensity until the end of the game. Using your self-talk to remind yourself of these goals is an excellent way to keep focused throughout a lopsided contest.

Sitting on the Bench

Basketball players never set the goal of making a basketball team and then sitting on the bench watching others play, yet, it happens to everyone. All players think of PT as "playing time" instead of "pine time." However, only five players can be on the court for a particular team at a time. Due to varying levels of playing ability, some players will play more than others.

> If you have to sit the bench, you can use the time to watch the movements of the player you will probably sub in for and observe what is and isn't working for him or her.

This means that players will sometimes have to sit and watch their teammates play. Because all players are going to experience this at some time or another, it is best to know what to do while you are there, regardless of how much time you spend on the bench.

Here are a couple of suggestions to make "pine time" more productive for you. Obviously one of the best ways to spend your time is to cheer on your teammates. To understand what your cheering may mean to them, all you have to do is realize how much it means to you to have your teammates cheer for you. Cheering also makes you an important part of the game.

Another suggestion is to watch the teammate on the court whom you would be most likely to substitute for. This can help you to "go to school" on what is working, and not working, for your team offensively and defensively. You may also be able to give your teammates advice that could help while they are playing. Your goal in these situations is to try to learn something while on the bench during every game. This, like cheering, allows you to help your team from the bench and keeps you actively focused on the game.

Your self-talk while sitting on the bench, especially for long periods, is critical in determining your attitude toward the team and your enjoyment of being on a basketball team. If you feel you are not going to see much playing time, it is very important that you focus on self-improvement during practices, becoming a team player, and staying positive. It can be easy to let your self-talk become negative while getting little playing time. When this begins to occur, you must recognize the negative self-talk is happening and stop it immediately. One way to break the habit of negative self-talk statements is to interrupt them and replace them with realistic, positive self-talk. When you find yourself beginning to think negatively, visualize a stop sign or say, "Stop" to yourself (see chapter 2), then replace the negative statement with a positive one. Following are some examples of negative self-talk changed into positive self-talk statements:

Changing Negative Statements to Positive Self-Talk

NEGATIVE	POSITIVE
1. I never get to play.	1. My time will come.
2. I'm not a valuable teammate.	2. I will help the team any way I can.
3. People think I can't play.	3. There are many people who would be proud to be on this team.
4. They don't need me.	4. I am an important part of this team. My role is important.
5. I'm not any good.	5. I'm getting better.
6. The coach doesn't like me.	6. I have to show coach more in practice.

*FUN*damental Points to Remember

1. By understanding more thoroughly the role of basketball officials, you can stay better focused on your basketball game.

2. Use imagery, cue words (e.g., reframing technique), and your concentration skills to deal with opposing fans.

3. Think only about basketball during your basketball practices or games. Allow yourself to deal with off-the-court situations at the appropriate time.

4. Basketball is only one part of your life. It is important to keep a healthy balance between playing basketball and the other areas in your life.

5. Recovery from injury requires both mental and physical rehabilitation. Your attitude toward the injury and rehabilitation process will have a significant impact on recovery.

6. Use self-talk to remind you of your game goals and keep you focused throughout a lopsided contest.

7. Make sitting on the bench more productive by cheering for and "going to school" on your teammates, and by using positive self-talk.

STAYING MOTIVATED

You are what you repeatedly do.

—Shaquille O'Neal (paraphrasing Aristotle) after winning the NBA Most Valuable Player award for the 1999–2000 season

Attitude Adjustment

The difference between a winner and a loser is a matter of inches, and a matter of attitude.

—Nancy Lieberman-Cline (2-time NCAA national champion, 1984 Women's American Basketball Association champion, member of gold-medal-winning team at the 1975 Pan-American Games and of the 1976 silver-medal-winning Olympic team)

SCOUTING REPORT -CHAPTER EIGHT-

You will read how to

1. Recognize two types of basketball motivation—personal and outside motivation.
2. Use setting and evaluating goals to keep you motivated.
3. Defend against and handle burnout.

Even the most enthusiastic basketball players or coaches will sometimes lack the normal level of motivation needed to perform up to their expectations. The best way to get through these tough situations is to realize this is a normal part of basketball. Like many other sports, basketball is a game of repetition. To improve, you must practice your skills over and over. This can become monotonous, boring, or uninteresting, which decreases your enthusiasm for playing the game. Of utmost importance is that you find a way to return to your proper mo-

> It is important to balance your personal motivations with the outside ones.

tivational level. One way to do this is to understand that motivation can be separated into two types: (a) personal motivation and (b) outside motivation. *Personal motivation* comes from your own individual reasons and desires to play basketball (e.g., love of the game, challenge of improving, thrill of competition). *Outside motivation* is composed of factors that others may use to motivate you (e.g., awards, scholarships, money, approval for success). All basketball players and coaches are energized by both types of motivation. You need a healthy balance of these two to keep you excited about playing hoops. Most players play hardest and enjoy basketball most when personal motivational factors are the strongest incentives. When you seek to improve and compete, rather than try to win an award, you find basketball is most enjoyable to play.

Therefore, when you find yourself going through a down period (where you enjoy basketball less than you normally do), you may need to examine your current motivations. Ask yourself, "Why am I really playing this sport? What attracts me to basketball? Am I emphasizing the correct aspects of the game that really interest me?" Many times, you will find the answers to these questions in your personal motivations to play basketball. To overcome a lack of motivation, you may need to use your positive self-talk to reemphasize your personal reasons for being a basketball participant and to de-emphasize the outside reasons for motivation. Remind yourself of the rewarding aspects (e.g., being with teammates, improving skills, staying in good physical shape) of playing the game that keep it fun for you. Many times, simply reminding yourself of why you love

> If you feel unmotivated, you may need to reexamine your reasons for playing basketball.

the game is enough to get you back into the swing of things. Think back to when you started playing basketball. What attracted you to the game in the first place?

I play this game because I love it.
—Sheryl Swoopes (4-time WNBA champion, Gold Medalist with the 1996 United States Women's Olympic basketball team, and 1993 NCAA national champion)

Goal Setting

Sometimes you may need to do more homework to revitalize your motivation for basketball. One assignment that will help you is to make a list of immediate, short-, and long-range goals that you would like to achieve. Although it can be helpful for the coach and the entire team to set overall team goals, you may set your own personal goals to help give you specific challenges and get you motivated again. (Goal setting can be helpful even if you are not having problems with your motivation.) For example, you can set goals for your endurance training, basketball practice, and games. When you set your goals, it is important that you come up with realistic, achievable goals that will challenge you, yet not be too difficult or easy. In the beginning, you may wish to set just a few reasonable goals. Once you get the hang of it, you may want to challenge yourself with more goals. If you find you have many goals you would like to work on to improve, you may find it helpful to prioritize your goals. By prioritizing your goals, you can determine which goals are most immediately important to you. The following are examples of some immediate, short-, and long-range goals that you could set for yourself:

You should try to set goals that are reasonable to achieve and measurable, as most of these goals are. For example, it can be quite easy to keep a record of your free-throw-shooting performance at practice with a daily chart. At the end of a chosen time period (i.e., week or month), you can check to see if you reached your goal.

Although a personal goal like "giving a good effort" is not as precisely measured as free-throw-shooting accuracy, you can

Endurance Training		
Immediate Goals	*Short-Range Goals*	*Long-Range Goals*
*Run 15 minutes today	*Run 25 minutes, 3 days per week	*Run 45 minutes, 4 days per week
*Weight training for 30 minutes today	*Weight training for 30 minutes, 2 days per week	*Weight training for 30 minutes, 3 days per week
Basketball Practice		
Immediate Goals	*Short-Range Goals*	*Long-Range Goals*
*Focus 100% today	*100% focus this week	*100% focus this month
*Shoot 50 free throws, making 35–40 today	*Shoot 50 free throws, making 35–40 at least 2 times per week	*Shoot 50 free throws, making 38–43 at least 4 times per week
Basketball Games		
Immediate Goals	*Short-Range Goals*	*Long-Range Goals*
*Get 5 assists in this game	*Average 5 assists per game this month	*Average 5 assists per game this season
*Give good effort today	*Give good effort this week	*Give good effort during the entire season

still develop your own rating system. For instance, at the end of each practice you could rate yourself from 1–10 (1 = *very poor effort*, 10 = *outstanding effort*) on a daily chart.

Again, at the end of a selected period, you may check to see if you reached your effort goals. If you find that you reach a goal much more quickly than you expected, readjust your goal so it will present a challenge to you. By the same means, if you have set a goal that is too difficult to reach, adjust it to a more reasonable level that will still challenge you.

Goal setting can be an excellent way to help you get your focus back, challenge you, and inspire you to reach new heights in basketball. By setting specific and measurable goals, you provide yourself with increased opportunities to experience personal achievement in playing basketball. The more personal achievements you can accomplish, the more likely you will keep your personal motivation to play at a high level. *A final note about goal setting*: It is highly suggested that you "ink your goals, don't just think them." In other words, once you set your goals, write or type them, and then place them where you will look over them frequently. This

Effort Rating
Sunday . . . . . Did not practice
Monday 7
Tuesday 8
Wednesday 6
Thursday 9
Friday 8
Saturday 7
Average Effort Rating = 7.5

> Set specific, measurable goals, and *write them down*.

will help you to more precisely remember what you have set out to do. Also remember that goal setting may be helpful for other areas in your life outside of basketball (e.g., schoolwork, job, family).

Ultimate Imagery

A great way to support the goals you have set is to tailor your imagery sessions to mentally practice reaching the goals you have set for yourself (improving free throw percentage, getting more rebounds, improving concentration, etc.). Also, a fun way some players like to use imagery is to envision reaching an important goal—an ultimate goal. For instance, many Olympic athletes report they stay motivated for their long training periods by using imagery to see and feel what it would be like to be standing on the Olympic stand with a gold medal around their necks while their national anthem is being played. You can use this technique to help you stay motivated for a long-range or ultimate goal. For example, some college coaches have their players use imagery to see and feel themselves winning a national basketball championship. (Some teams actually practice what their on-court celebration would be like if they won the championship!) Using imagery in this way is an excellent and fun way to keep yourself motivated to reach one of your ultimate goals. Use ultimate imagery any time you feel you need a motivational boost.

Avoiding and Dealing With Burnout

An extreme loss of motivation to play or coach basketball may result in burnout. Burnout occurs when a participant no longer feels rewarded by playing or coaching basketball. A person who is experiencing basketball burnout has no desire to play or coach. If such people force themselves to do so, they usually just "go through the motions," showing few, if any, emotions. For instance, burned-out players may shoot 25 free throws at the end of practice, but they do not care how many they make. They may show a lackadaisical attitude about their performance. Burnout has become a common phenomenon today because there really is no off-season for many basketball players and coaches. Even when their actual playing season is over, many are required to continue (or it is strongly suggested that they continue) involvement throughout the year. Burnout occurs because participants are not receiving mean-

ingful rewards, and they need a mental and physical time-out from the sport. A person experiencing total burnout feels mentally, physically, and emotionally exhausted.

The best way to deal with burnout is "preventive medicine." This means you should try to keep burnout from occurring. One way to do this is to enjoy the off-season with another sport or at least spend some time away from basketball. Be sure to let your body and mind rest from basketball for a significant time after each season. Even during the season, do not let basketball consume your whole life. Although it may be your top priority, you must and need to give attention to the other areas of your life to maintain a balanced existence. In your life, basketball has its place, but it must be kept in proper perspective. Although basketball may be very important to you, it is NOT a "life-or-death" situation. Also, write down and think about the rewarding aspects of playing or coaching the game. It is important that you feel rewarded for playing or coaching basketball in order to see the benefits of participating.

If you find that you get to the point of total burnout, taking an extended break from the sport may be all that you can do. If you try to continue while totally burned out, you run the risk of making playing basketball a miserable experience for you. If you feel you must continue, do your best to emphasize the things about the game you enjoy. It may also be helpful to work

PREVENTIVE MEDICINE FOR BURNOUT

- Play another sport or take time off from basketball during the off-season.
- Let your mind and body rest for a significant time after the end of the season.
- Don't let basketball consume your entire life during the season.
- Write down and think about the rewarding aspects of playing basketball.

with a sport psychologist or counselor. You may find a competent sport psychologist or counselor by asking others who have experienced burnout, by searching the Web, or by looking in the telephone book. The Association for the Advancement of Applied Sport Psychology (AAASP) has a Web site (http://www.aaasponline.org) to help you locate AAASP-certified sport psychologists in your area.

Remember, even one of the greatest basketball players of all time, Michael Jordan, took a needed break from the sport he so loved. Even though taking a break may not be the most convenient action for you at the time (especially if it is during the playing season), in the long run it may be just the "medicine" that is needed to revive your love for the game.

*FUN*damental Points to Remember

1. Motivation can be separated into two types: personal and outside motivation.

2. To overcome a lack of motivation, you may need to use your positive self-talk to reemphasize your personal reasons for playing or coaching basketball, while de-emphasizing the outside reasons for motivation.

3. Try setting immediate, short-, and long-range goals to keep or improve motivation.

4. Prioritize your goals to determine which goals have the most immediate importance to you.

5. Develop your own rating system to evaluate your progress toward reaching goals that are more difficult to measure, such as effort, attitude, and concentration level.

6. Tailor your imagery sessions to mentally practice reaching the goals you have set.

7. Use "ultimate imagery" as a fun way to keep yourself motivated to reach long-range goals.

8. The best way to handle burnout is to keep it from occurring—preventive medicine.

9. The Association for the Advancement of Applied Sport Psychology (AAASP) has a Web site

   (www.aaasponline.org)

   to help you locate AAASP-certified sport psychologists in your area.

9

GAINING AND MAINTAINING CONFIDENCE

It's human nature to have doubts. It's how you deal with them that matters.

—Kobe Bryant (2000 NBA World Champion Los Angeles Lakers, before the sixth game of the 2000 NBA finals against the Indiana Pacers)

In the next three years, I will be one of the best players in the league.

—Rebecca Lobo (Star in the WNBA, member of the 1996 Olympic Gold Medal team and of the undefeated (35-0) University of Connecticut 1995 NCAA national championship team)

SCOUTING REPORT
-CHAPTER NINE-

You will read how to

1. Gain and maintain your confidence.
2. Handle "pressure" situations successfully.
3. Use "present-moment, task-focused thinking" to help you perform well.

Losing Confidence

One of the best ways to understand how to regain your confidence is to first understand exactly how you lose your confidence. Many players believe they lose their confidence due to one or a series of bad performances. This is not entirely true. The poor performances do not cause you to lose your confidence. *YOU* are the cause of your lost or diminished confidence. More precisely, what you think after bad performances

> A poor performance doesn't cause you to lose confidence, but the way you think about it can.

is what causes you to lose your confidence. Negative self-talk drains your confidence to a low level. Many players develop a negative thought habit that occurs almost every time games or practices do not go their way. They begin thinking or saying to themselves such things as "I can't guard her/him," "I'll probably miss this free throw, " or "I can't make a jump shot." What occurs then is what is known as a self-fulfilling prophecy. Because their self-talk is negative, their basketball performance remains poor. Because their performance is still poor, they continue with the negative self-statements. Unless the player does something to change it, this can be a never-ending cycle of negative events—a performance slump.

Gaining Confidence

Unfortunately, many players simply hope and wait for a good performance to occur to break the negative cycle of thinking and playing. However, with their thought patterns really serving as a self-defeating (or playing-defense-on-themselves) mechanism, this can cause an extended playing slump. If you find yourself in this negative habit of thinking, remind yourself of this true, three-step logic. As mentioned in chapter 2,

1. Your confidence comes from your self-talk or what YOU think about yourself.
2. YOU are in control of what you think and say to yourself (self-talk).

3. Therefore, YOU ARE IN CONTROL OF YOUR CONFIDENCE.

Once you realize that you are in control of your confidence, it is much easier to regain it. Rather than having to wait on happenstance to restore your confidence, you have the power to restore it yourself. For example, have you ever wondered how some team scorers can miss their first 7–8 shots (or more) yet keep "firing" away at the basket? Although you may hear some well-meaning observers state that they must have "no conscience," what is really true is that most good scorers remain confident. They feel that no matter how many shots they miss in a row, the next shot will go in, or they will "get hot" soon. Instead of engaging in pessimistic self-talk such as "I can't seem to make anything" or "It's not my night," they instead use more optimistic self-talk such as "I will make the next shot" or "My team needs me to score." By using this type of more positive self-talk (gem talk), you can help yourself to break out of a performance slump much sooner than you can by just hoping and waiting for it to happen. What is more important, you learn that you are in control of how you think, which has a big influence on how you perform. You are who you are because you have chosen to be that way.

Imagery can also help to put you back on the road to more positive thinking. You may use imagery sessions to see yourself performing as you want to perform. Sometimes coaches or players will watch an actual game videotape of some past good performance to help them see themselves performing well, in order to build confidence. In the same manner, imagery may be used to help you to mentally experience and see yourself performing well, which can help to regain your confidence.

Also, imagery is an excellent way to get you into the habit of thinking more optimistically after a poor performance. Let's say you miss five free throws in a row near the end of the first half. At half-time you could image, thinking to yourself confidence-keeping statements like "That's OK. I'll make the next one" or "I'll stay calm because I know I am a good free throw shooter." In this case, you are using imagery to develop a positive mental habit of remaining confident. In this way, imagery may be used to develop and practice more positive thought habits.

Dealing With Pressure

We like pressure. I know I thrive on it.

—Bill Walton (Hall of Famer, 2-time NBA champion; and star of the UCLA men's basketball teams, which won 86 of 90 games and two NCAA national championships)

Near the end of the championship game, you have been fouled while dribbling near the top, but inside of, the three-point arc. Your team is behind by one point, and there is no time left on the game clock. You are sent to the free throw line with no teammates or opponents lined up along the lane lines. If you make the first free throw, the game will be tied. Your team will then either go into an overtime period (if you miss the second free throw) or win the game (if you make the second free throw). However, if you miss the first free throw, then your team will lose the game. This is a pressure situation, right? *Not necessarily!* It depends on what you think of it. Again, your self-talk determines what you think about this situation and how

> You can avoid pressure situations by thinking optimistic, calm thoughts.

you react to it. Remember this fact: "*There is no such thing as a pressure situation. A situation is determined by what you think of it.*" This statement means that a situation only becomes a pressure situation if you think of it that way. All pressure is self-imposed. As mentioned earlier in this chapter, you are in control of what you think. You can *choose* to think differently (optimistically) to help you perform better. A more realistic and positive approach to thinking about this situation is to label this situation, and others like it, as "challenging" situations. If you label a situation like the one in the free throw example as a pressure situation, you are likely to have negative thoughts such as "The pressure is on me now," "I hope I don't choke and let the team down," or "If I don't make both of these free throws and we lose, then I lost the game." To be able to more productively label the free throw situation as challenging, you must remind yourself that even if you miss the first or second free throw, and your team loses, you *never* lose a game by yourself. Realistically, there are numerous plays (i.e., missed shots, other missed free throws, turnovers, lack of rebounding, poor defense) that occur in a basketball game. No one play or player is the sole reason for a loss. For any player to label him-/herself, or another player, as the only reason a game is lost is incorrect and unfair. You may hear others say that a "crucial" play or player won the game. The reality is that it takes all the plays and all the players to win (or lose) a game.

With this realization in mind, you can more easily take the pressure off yourself. You may think of this free throw situation in the following manner: "This is exactly where I want to be. I want the opportunity to make these free throws. This is why I play basketball, to be in fun and exciting situations like these. I love the challenge!"

This kind of gem talk will give you more of an opportunity to be successful, under little or no self-administered pressure. Even if you were to miss one or both of the free throws, you would realize that the game was lost by the entire team, not just by you. Learning to label situations like these as "fun" can have a positive impact on your performance. Always keep in mind that you will succumb to pressure only if you talk yourself into it!

Another tactic that can help keep you from thinking about pressure situations is to manipulate your concentration. In the free throw example, this would mean once you get to the line and are ready to shoot, you would use the few-outside focus to focus on the rim. In many cases, if you can change the focus of your concentration to "zero in" on the present (instead of what happened in the past or what may happen in the future) and what you are supposed to do, this will prevent you from thinking self-defeating thoughts. This type of present-moment, task-focused thinking should help you to perform well in these challenging situations.

Imagery can also be used to help you to get into the habit of labeling situations as challenging. With imagery you can mentally practice both the proper mental and the proper physical responses to challenging situations. You can mentally rehearse thinking the proper and positive self-talk necessary to help you perform effectively. Again, imagery can be an important practice strategy to help you develop both positive thinking habits and successful physical-performance techniques.

*FUN*damental Points to Remember

1. What you think causes you to lose your confidence. Negative self-talk lowers your confidence level.

2. Because your confidence comes from what you think, and you control what you think, you can control your confidence.

3. Use imagery to develop a positive mental habit of remaining confident.

4. There is no such thing as a pressure situation. A situation is determined by what you think of it. Therefore, all pressure is self-imposed.

5. Learning to label situations as "fun" or "challenging" can have a positive impact on your basketball performance.

6. Present-moment, task-focused thinking should help you to perform well in challenging situations.

7. Imagery can help you mentally practice both the proper mental and the proper physical responses to challenging situations.

10

PLAYING IN THE FUN ZONE

Be strong in body, clean in mind, lofty in ideals.
—James Naismith

Getting the Most From Playing Basketball

The sport of basketball offers many challenges and opportunities for excitement. It is a sport enjoyed by all ages, and besides being one of the most popular sports today, basketball is an activity that you may enjoy for a lifetime. Whether you want to become a professional, college, high school, good "noontime" or "pick-up game" player, or simply want to improve on your skills, acquiring the proper knowledge of both the mental and physical skills of "round ball" is a necessity. These skills are

SCOUTING REPORT -CHAPTER TEN-

You will read how to

1. Realize that mental and physical basketball skills go hand in hand: They are inseparable.
2. Make the *FUN*damental skills even more valuable to you in areas of your life beyond the sport of basketball.
3. Become your own best teammate or coach.

inseparable and go hand in hand. Emphasizing only the physical skills in basketball is similar to a point guard's knowing how to dribble, shoot, and pass, but not knowing the appropriate time to perform each of these activities. This book began by stating that to truly succeed in basketball, you need 100% physical skills and 100% effort in mental skills. To make dramatic and drastic improvements and be the best player you can become, you must emphasize BOTH. It is important to practice both mental and physical skills. Most coaches and players state that the mental side of basketball is worth at least 50% (many give higher percentages, such as 75–90%) of playing the game. It is up to you to take the next step to answer this *FUN*damental question: How much time will you devote to improving and maintaining the mental side of your basketball skills? By reading and applying the techniques of the *FUN*damental skills provided to you in this book, you have taken the first step to becoming a true all-round player. It is now up to you to put this critical knowledge to good use and give yourself a PRIME-TIME ASSIST.

Any team can be a miracle team, but you have to go out and work for your miracles.
—Pat Riley (NBA head coach of the Miami Heat and former head coach of four NBA championship teams with the Los Angeles Lakers)

Applying Your Basketball Skills to Life

Like life, basketball is messy and unpredictable. It has its way with you, no matter how hard you try to control it. In basketball, as in life, true joy comes from being fully present in each and every moment...
—Phil Jackson (Head coach of eight NBA championship teams, six with the Chicago Bulls and two with the Los Angeles Lakers, and member of the 1973 NBA champion New York Knicks.)

Although it is important to learn the *FUN*damental skills to become a more proficient basketball player or coach, these mental techniques would be underused if you did not apply them to other significant areas of your life. Imagery, concentration techniques, and positive self-talk can be even more valuable to

you in areas outside of the basketball arena. They can have a dramatic and drastic impact on your well-being and success. The number of situations and circumstances that the *FUN*da-

> Imagery, concentration, and self-talk can be applied to countless other areas of your life.

mental skills may help you in are endless, and are limited only by your creativity. Knowing where and how to focus your concentration is critical in taking any written test, reading, driving a car, listening, communicating, etc.,—any task that requires you to pay attention to what you are doing or what may be going on around you. Imagery may be used for building your confidence for job interviews, taking tests in school, improving your social skills, preparing for a presentation, relaxing, or practicing your concentration. Let's say that you grow very nervous before and during interviews. The *FUN*damental skills can help you deal with this type of encounter. In preparation for the interview, you can use imagery to help you see yourself looking and feeling professional during the interview. By knowing how to focus your concentration, you will be able to listen appropriately and prepare to answer the forthcoming questions. Positive self-talk will keep you confident throughout the interview.

Training yourself to have more optimistic self-talk may be the most important of these *FUN*damental skills. Your self-statements and thoughts are the foundation of how you act, react, and perform in daily life. Most important, your self-talk determines your happiness, enjoyment (or lack thereof), and ability to handle the challenging uncertainties that life presents you. As you should do in basketball, do in life—BE YOUR OWN BEST TEAMMATE.

An optimist is one who sees an opportunity in every difficulty: a pessimist is one who sees a difficulty in every opportunity.
—Abraham Lincoln (The 16th President of the United States of America)

*FUN*damental Points to Remember

1. Basketball is an activity that you may enjoy for a lifetime and that offers many challenges and opportunities for excitement.

2. The proper knowledge of both the mental and the physical skills of basketball is a necessity, because these skills are inseparable.

3. Imagery, concentration techniques, and positive self-talk can be even more valuable to you in areas of life outside of basketball.

4. Your self-statements and thoughts are the foundation of how you act, react, and perform in daily life.

5. Self-talk determines your happiness, enjoyment (or lack thereof), and ability to handle the challenging uncertainties that life presents you.

6. BE YOUR OWN BEST TEAMMATE OR COACH.

APPENDIX

RELATED WEB SITES

Basketball-Related Web Sites

International Basketball Federation
www.fiba.com/fs_main.asp

National Collegiate Athletic Association
www.ncaabasketball.net

Continental Basketball Association
www.cbahoops.com

Basketball Hall of Fame
www.hoophall.com/index.cfm

National Junior College Athletic Association
www.njcaa.org

Women's Basketball Coaches Association
www.wbca.org

National Federation of State High School Associations
www.nfhs.org/index.htm

National Basketball Association
www.nba.com

National Wheelchair Basketball Association
www.nwba.org/index2.html

United States Basketball League
www.usbl.com

Women's National Basketball Association
www.wnba.com

Women's Basketball Hall of Fame
www.wbhof.com

American Athletic Association of the Deaf, Inc.
www.usadb.org

National Association of Intercollegiate Athletics
www.naia.org

National Association of Basketball Coaches
www.nabc.com

Amateur Athletic Union
www.aausports.org/ysnim/home/aau_index.jsp

Harlem Globetrotters
www.harlemglobetrotters.com

International Association of Approved Basketball Officials
www.iaabo.org

Dr. Kevin L. Burke's Web Sites:

Dr. Burke's personal Web site
www.kevinlburke.com

Dr. Burke's sport psychology Web site
www.sport-psychology.com

INDEX

A

Association for the Advancement of Applied Sport Psychology (AAASP), 93

B

Barry, Rick, 40

basketball, xiii–xiv. *See also* basketball, and mental skills; basketball players, and dealing with specific situations; basketball skills, application to life situations; confidence; defense; FUNdamental skills; motivation; shooting

coaches, xiv–xv, 78–79

getting the most from playing, 103–4

improving all-around as a player

skill correction, 59–60

skill improvement, 55–56, 58–59

and slumps, 59–60

and using the "off" hand, 60–63

and parents, xv–xvi

players, xiv

basketball, and mental skills, 3, 5–8, 33. *See also* FUNdamental skills, mental practice

basketball players, and dealing with specific situations

being benched, 82–83

coaches, 78–79

injury and rehabilitation, 79–81

mental rehabilitation, 80

losing, 81

officials, 74–76

off-the-court, 77–78

opposing fans, 76–77

teammates, 78–79

basketball skills, application to life situations, 104, 106

basketball-related web sites, 109–10

Bird, Larry, 4

Brown, Dale, 28

Bryant, Kobe, 95

burnout. *See* motivation, and burnout

C

concentration. *See* FUNdamental skills, concentration awareness

concentration flexibility, 23

confidence, 95

and dealing with pressure, 99–101

gaining, 96, 98

losing, 96

D

defense

and mental skills for improving, 47–48

one-on-one, 50–51

team, 48, 50

using self-talk to improve, 51–53

zone, 48

E

endurance training chart, 88

F

free throws. *See* shooting, free throws

FUNdamental points to remember, 8, 33, 45, 53, 63, 72, 84, 94, 101, 107

FUNdamental skills, xiv, xv–xvi, 4–5, 37, 42, 56, 68, 70–71, 104, 106:

#1 / mental practice, 10, 12

    getting started, 13–14

    notebook, 15–16

    schedule, 15

    understanding, 12–13

    when to practice, 14–15

#2 / concentration awareness, 19–20, 58–59, 60

    four ways to focus, 21–22, 23

        few-inside (FI), 21, 39

        few-outside (FO), 21–22, 27, 39–40

        many-inside (MI), 21

        many-outside (MO), 21

    full-court, 24

    practice, 25–28

    specifics, 20–21

    three aspects of, 22–24

    and time-outs, 24–25

    tips, 24–25

    understanding, 20

3# / positive self-talk (gem talk), 28–29, 59, 83, 100. *See also* defense, using self-talk to improve

    and changing thought habits, 29–32

    self-talk statements, 31

    and sense of humor, 32

G

goal-setting, 89–90

gem talk. *See* FUNdamental skills #3 / positive self-talk

I

imagery, 18–19, 33, 38–39, 56, 58, 71, 98

   and belief, 18

   and control, 18

   imagery FAQs, 16–18

   and injuries, 79–81

   practicing, 14

   "quick," 42–43

   and viewpoint, 17–18

J

Jackson, Phil, 104

Jordan, Michael, 10, 19, 55, 93

K

Knight, Bob, 4

L

Leslie, Lisa, 12, 32

Lieberman-Cline, Nancy, 85

Lincoln, Abraham, 106

Lobo, Rebecca, 95

M

mental practice. *See* FUNdamental skills #1 / mental practice

Mental Practice Notebook (MPN), 15–16

mental rehabilitation imagery scenario, 80

mental stimulation, 26

motivation
   attitude adjustment, 85–87
   and burnout, 90, 92–93
      positive medicine for, 92
   and goal-setting, 87–90
   outside, 86
   personal, 86
   and ultimate imagery, 90

N
Naismith, James, 65, 103

O
O'Neal, Shaquille, 32, 85

P
Price, Mark, 42

R
rebound statements, 30–31
relaxation training, 26
Riley, Pat, 104
Russell, Bill, 12

S
self-talk. *See* FUNdamental skills #3 / positive self-talk
shooting, 17
   and basket interference, 37
   and concentration, 39–40
   free throws, 5
      mental routine for, 40–45
      physical routine for, 44–45

and imagery practice, 38–39

sporting behavior. *See also* trash talking

being a good sport, 65–66

and emotional control, 70–71

and the three-seconds rule, 71

and psych-out attempts, 69–70

Stockton, John, 32

Summitt, Pat, 8, 32

Swoopes, Sheryl, 87

T

trash talk, 28, 66–69

dealing with, 68

and special trash-talk practice, 69

W

Walton, Bill, 99

Wooden, John, 8, 77